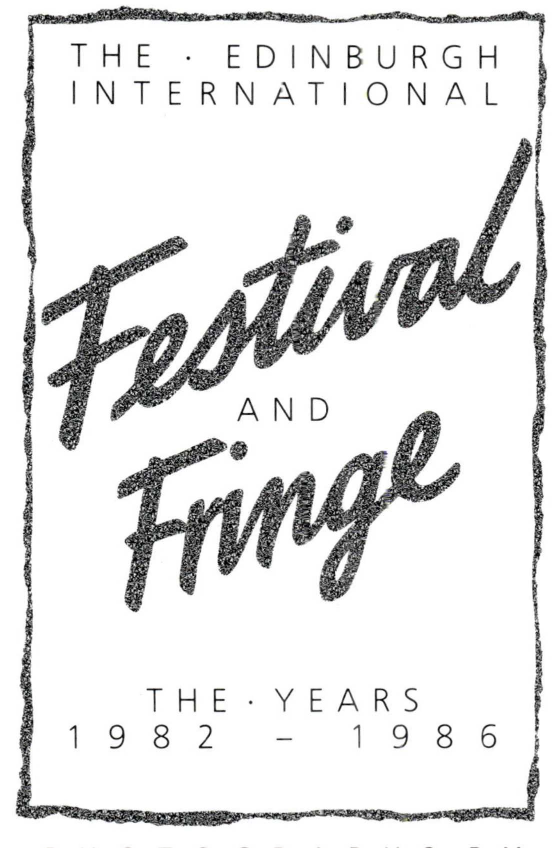

THE EDINBURGH INTERNATIONAL FESTIVAL AND FRINGE

THE YEARS 1982 – 1986

PHOTOGRAPHS BY
MARIUS ALEXANDER

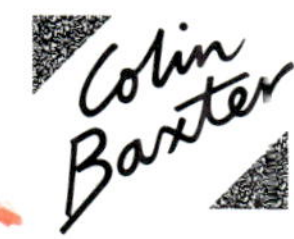

First published in Great Britain in 1987 by
Colin Baxter Photography Ltd.
Lamington, Biggar, Lanarkshire, ML12 6HW

British Library Cataloguing in Publication Data
Alexander, Marius
The Edinburgh international festival and fringe:
the years 1982-1986.
1. Performing arts festivals—Scotland—
Edinburgh (Lothian)—Pictorial works
I. Title
700'.7'94134 GT4845.E3

ISBN 0-948661-02-X

Designed by Charles Miller Graphics, Edinburgh
Printed by Frank Peters Printers Ltd., Kendal, Cumbria

Biographical Note

Marius Alexander was born in 1953. He took up photography in 1975, as an adjunct to painting while living in London. During this period he made four extended photographic trips to the tribal areas of North Pakistan, before returning to Edinburgh in 1980. Marius now works freelance and his work has been widely published and exhibited.

FRONT COVER / SANKAI JUKU / 1982 / BACK COVER / BHUTTO DANCE COMPANY / 1982

THE FESTIVAL

1986 saw the fortieth anniversary of the Edinburgh Festival—the biggest, and many consider the best, all-round arts festival in the world. It may be less exclusive than, say, the Salzburg Festival, but this in itself is a large part of Edinburgh's appeal. For three weeks each summer Scotland's beautiful but rather sedate capital comes to life in a frenzy of artistic activity which includes just about everything from the sublime to the plainly ridiculous.

Before the first Festival it was a different story. Edinburgh barely existed on the cultural map of the forties and could not begin to compete with the likes of Paris, New York, or London in attracting the big names in the arts. It was an era of ration books and hard times, when trams clanged their way along Princes Street and culture was represented by the gathering of a handful of Scottish poets in the pubs of Rose Street. Art lovers interested in more than Christmas pantomimes or amateur operatics must have been tempted to emigrate.

The early Festivals changed all that. Suddenly local audiences found Bruno Walter, Kathleen Ferrier, Margot Fonteyn, and other great names on their doorstep. They could see Eliot's 'Cocktail Party' or the Scots classic 'The Thrie Estaites' presented by the outstanding actors and directors of that generation; they could visit Rembrandt and Gaugin exhibitions; and they could attend an open-air performance of Handel's 'Music for Royal Fireworks', with an accompanying fireworks display, in the imposing setting of the castle. The Festival was an immediate hit and it has remained so, with public and critics alike, to the present day.

The first Festival also attracted an unofficial or 'fringe' entry in the form of eight theatre companies who arrived uninvited, hired their own halls, and organised their own publicity. The Fringe has been with us ever since. By the end of the fifties some thirty groups were participating, a box office had been opened, a programme published, and a 'Fringe Club' started. By its very presence this off-shoot helped to shield the Festival from the tags of 'exclusive' and 'highbrow'.

Gradually the Fringe gained a reputation as a proving ground for new talent. It was cheap, accessible, and frequently controversial. It brought individuals like Jonathan Miller, Alan Bennett, and Tom Stoppard into the public eye for the first time; it was instrumental in establishing the Traverse Theatre and the Demarco Gallery; and in recent years it has provided a platform in Europe for the arts of many diverse cultures — one thinks particularly of the Japanese contribution to theatre and multi-media art, and the political impact of Black African theatre and music. As it has expanded, the Fringe has become a focal point of global culture, a unique arena for the exchange of ideas.

The Fringe is now as big an attraction as the official Festival. In 1980 alone 180 world premieres were staged. By 1986 the original eight shows had swelled to 900; almost half a million tickets were sold, and about 90,000 people turned out for 'Fringe Sunday' in Holyrood Park. This last event really sums up what the Fringe is about nowadays—in part a hangover from the alternative life-styles of the sixties; partly a vehicle for the new, the experimental, and the outrageous; and partly an excuse for having a good time.

As the years pass, the official Festival tends to incorporate elements once associated with the Fringe. It now includes many more experimental works in its programme, and has begun to stage performances in areas beyond the city centre. The Fringe, on the other hand, has learned a few tricks of its own. It is now a highly efficient organisation, with improved facilities, and an ability to attract companies and individuals whose reputations are already well-established. It is still capable of throwing up a few surprises, and, it must be said, a fair number of genuine turkeys, but something of its spontaneity has been lost in the rush to balance the books and give the public what it wants.

Despite, or perhaps because of this, the irrepressible spirit of the Fringe has resurfaced in a new form. In the early eighties competition for venues and audiences became so intense that many visiting performers took their acts onto the streets. Here they could reach an instant audience and cover their costs more effectively than in some dingy basement in the middle of nowhere. Jugglers, pavement artists, buskers, fire-eaters, comedians and many others now add their own boisterous contribution to the Festival City. At first the authorities tried to resist this contravention of the statutes, but to no avail. It takes more than a bye-law to suppress the spirit of the Fringe.

Marius Alexander's photographs of the years 1982-86 chronicle this transformation. They capture the fleeting moments, the odd-ball characters, the occasionally bemused spectators, and the bizarre situations to be found at the fringe of the Fringe. Other elements are here too, but this is not intended to be an all-embracing view. It is simply an opportunity to savour a few of the many ingredients which go into the vast melting pot known as the Edinburgh Festival.

Alan Edwards, 1987

FRINGE SUNDAY | HOLYROOD PARK | 1986

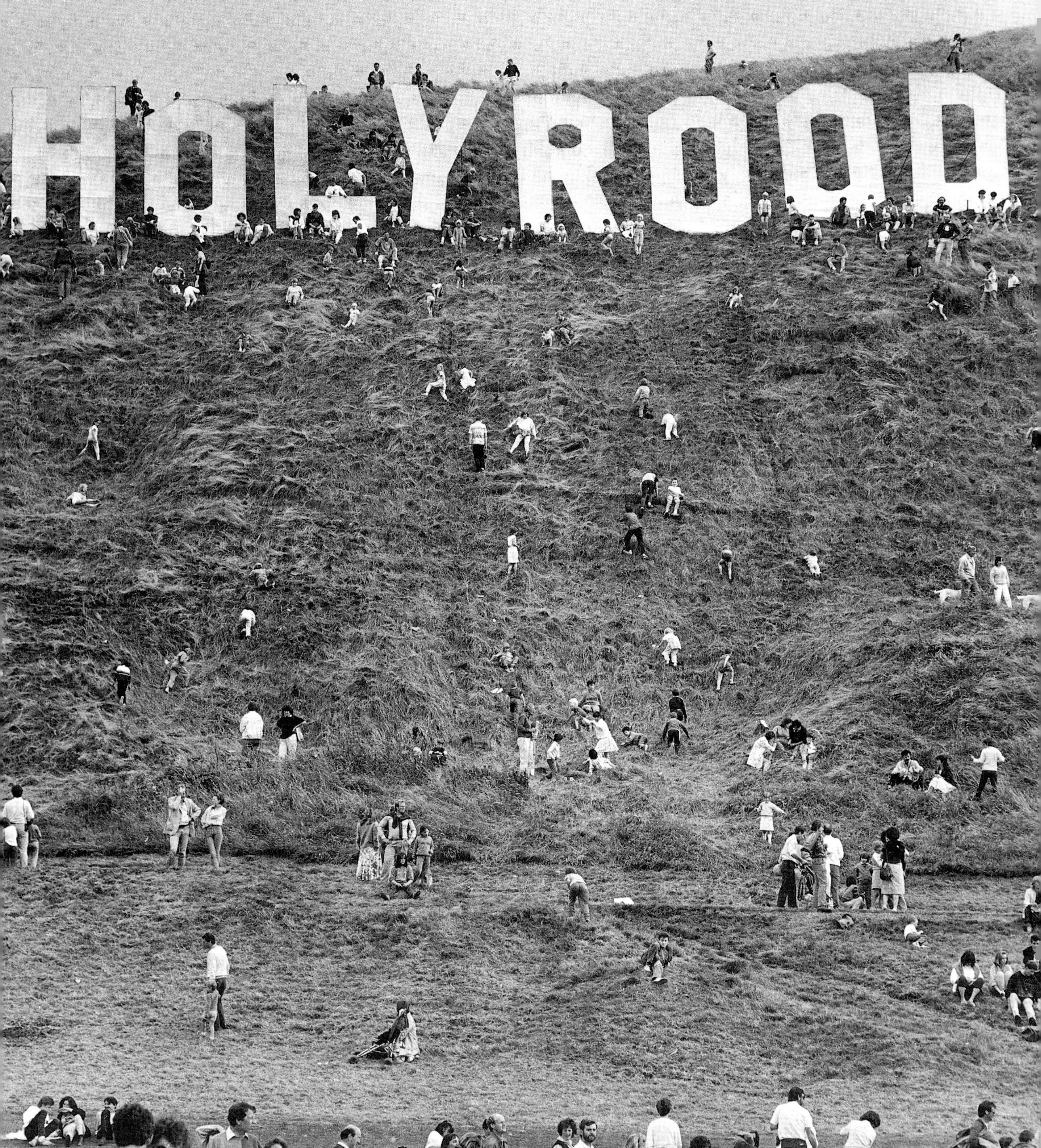
HOLYROOD

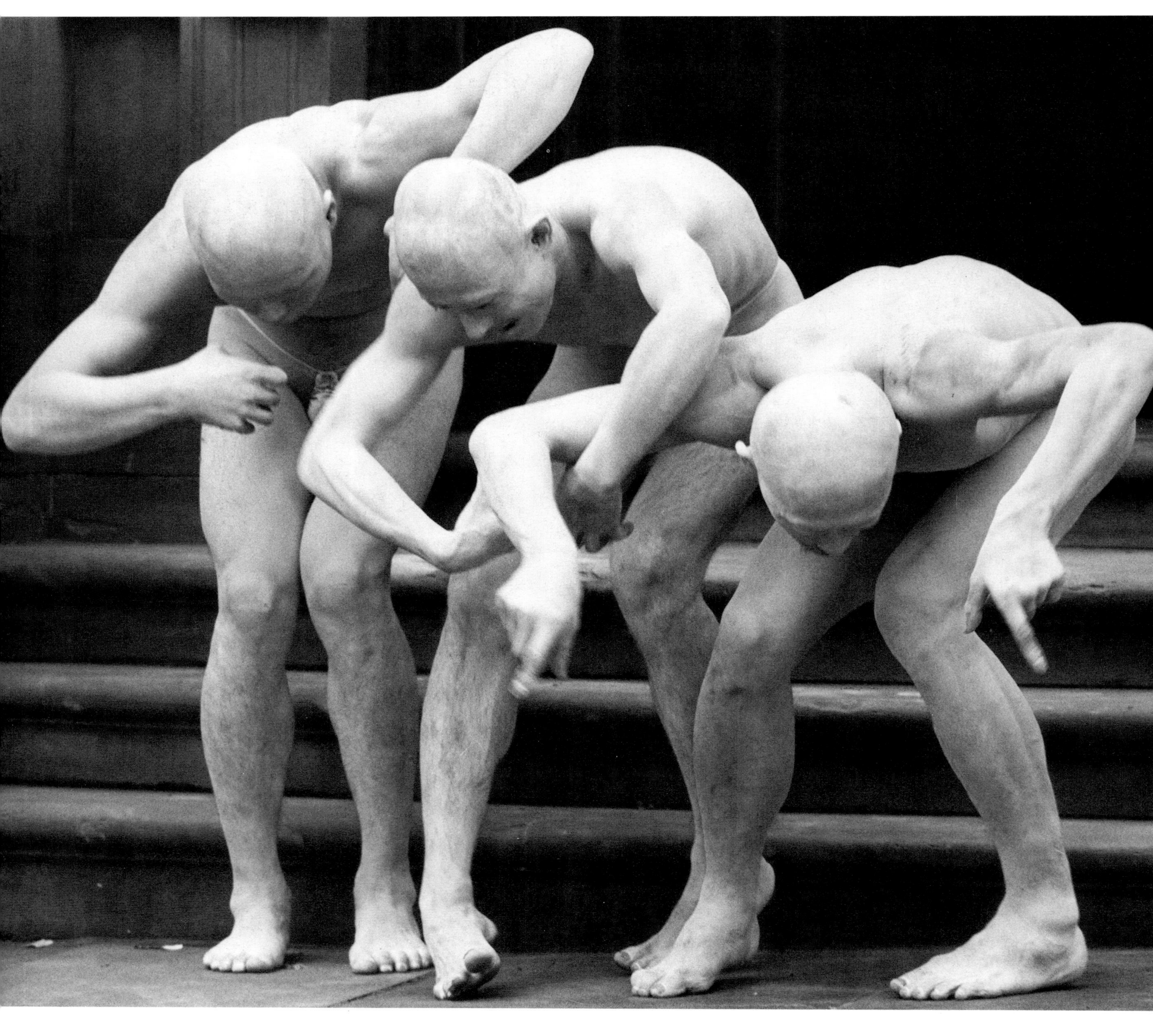

SANKAI JUKU THEATRE COMPANY | 1982

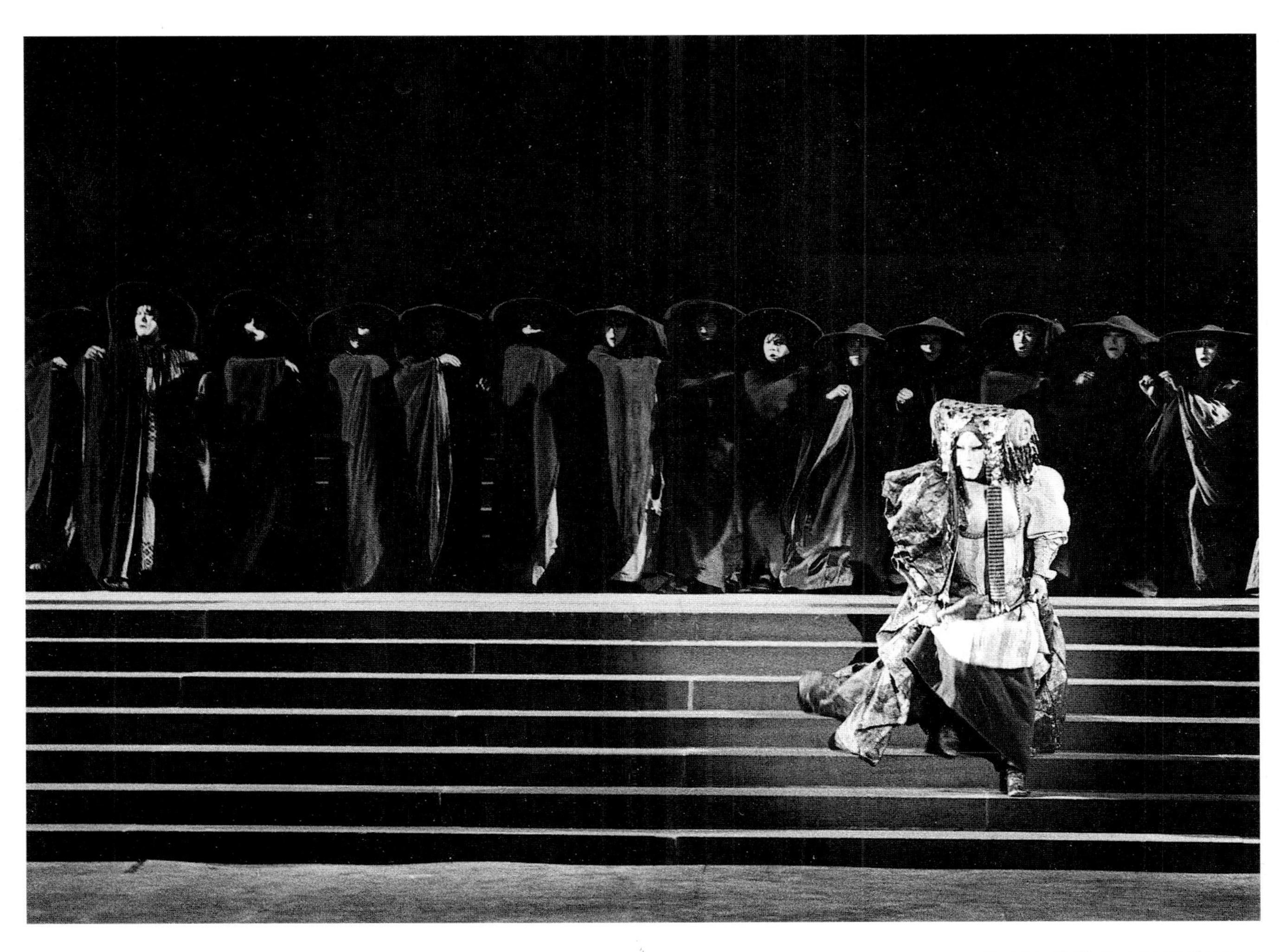

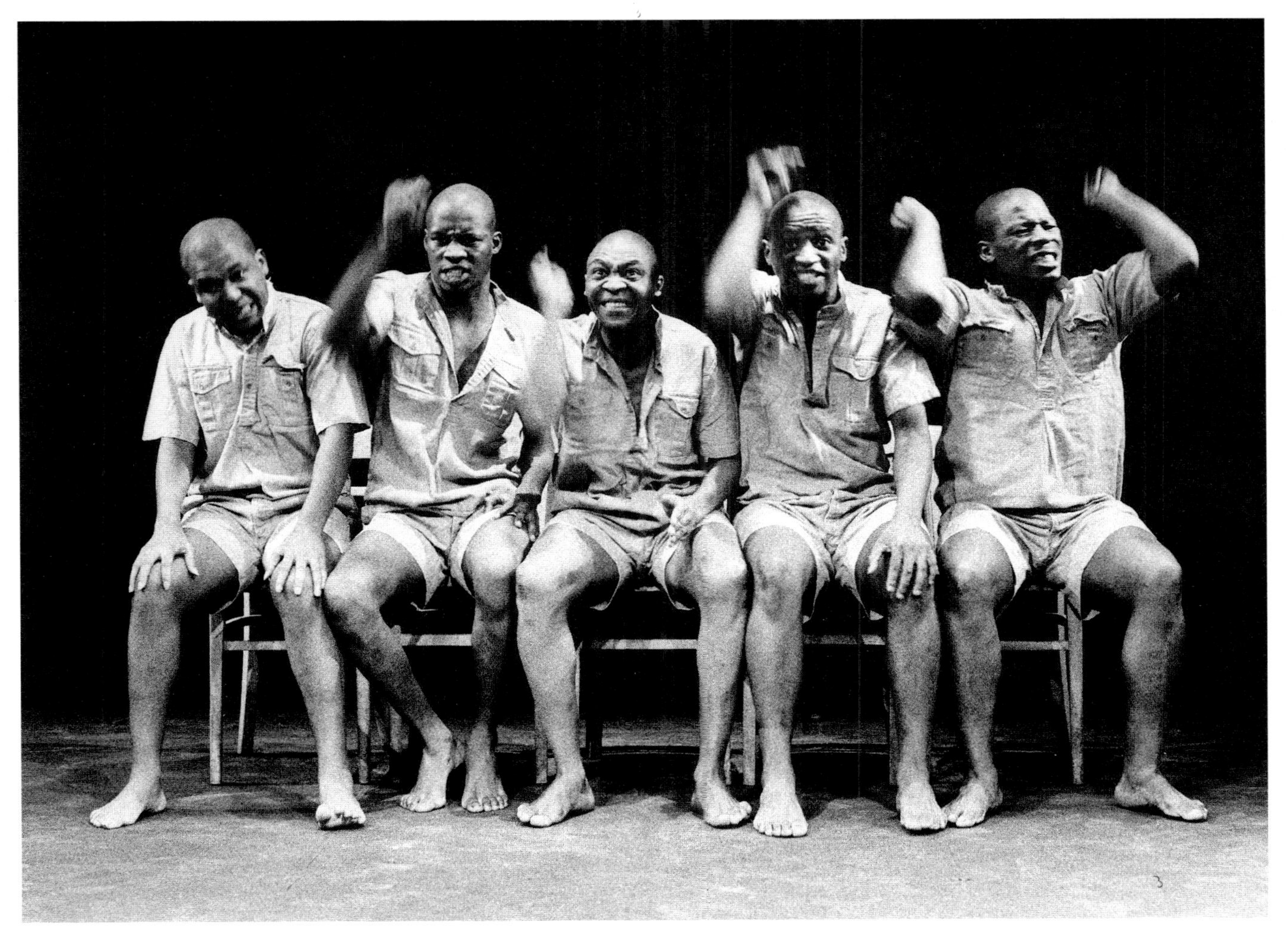

'MEDEA' | TOHO COMPANY OF JAPAN | 1986 | TOP

'BORN IN THE RSA' | MARKET THEATRE OF JOHANNESBURG | 1986

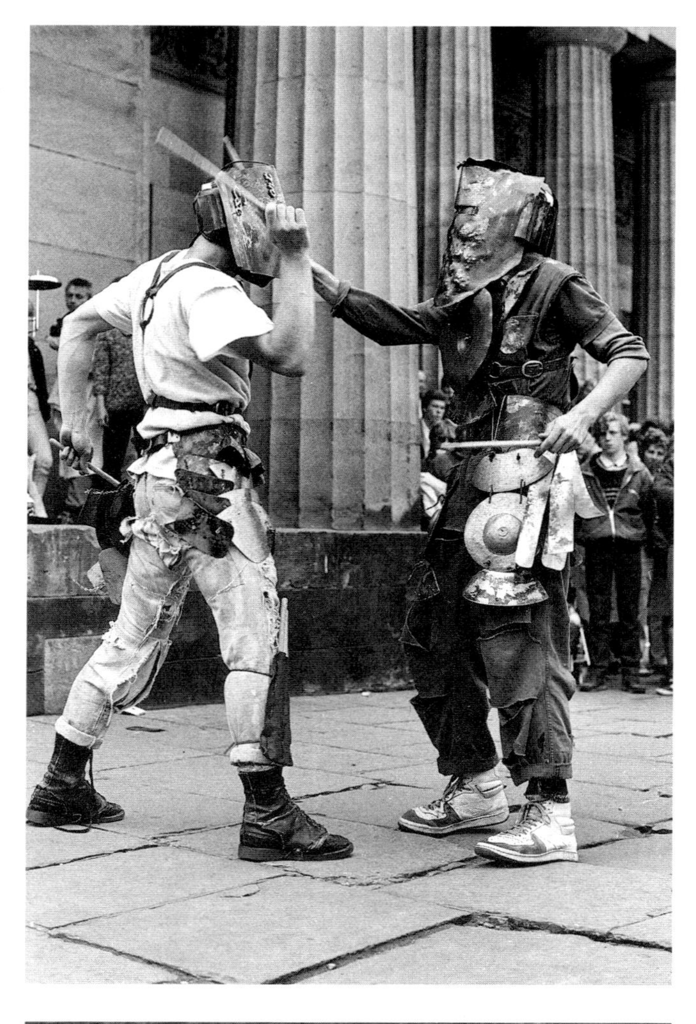

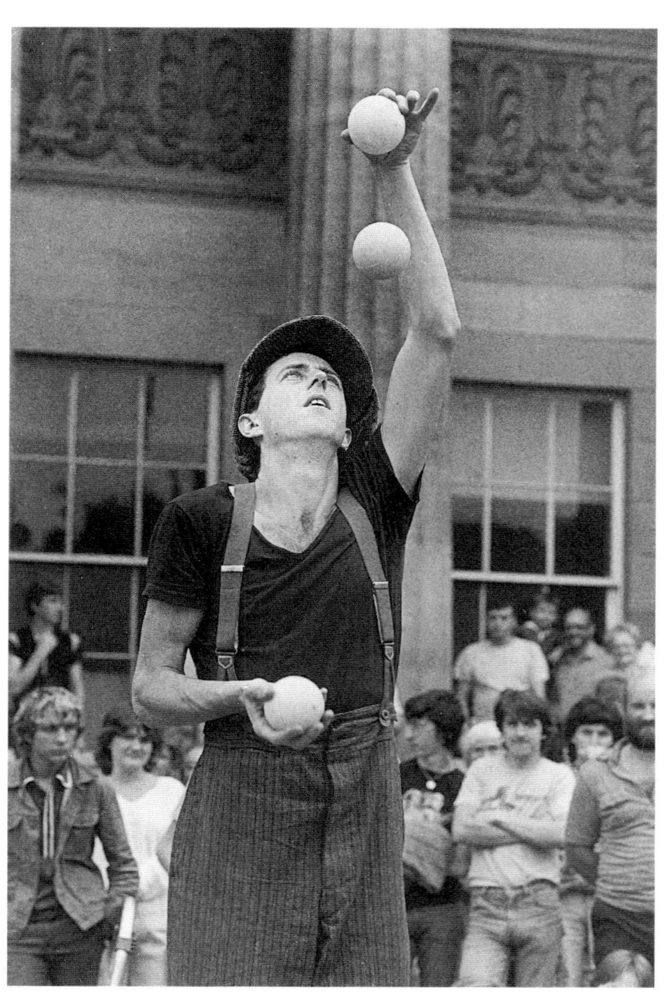

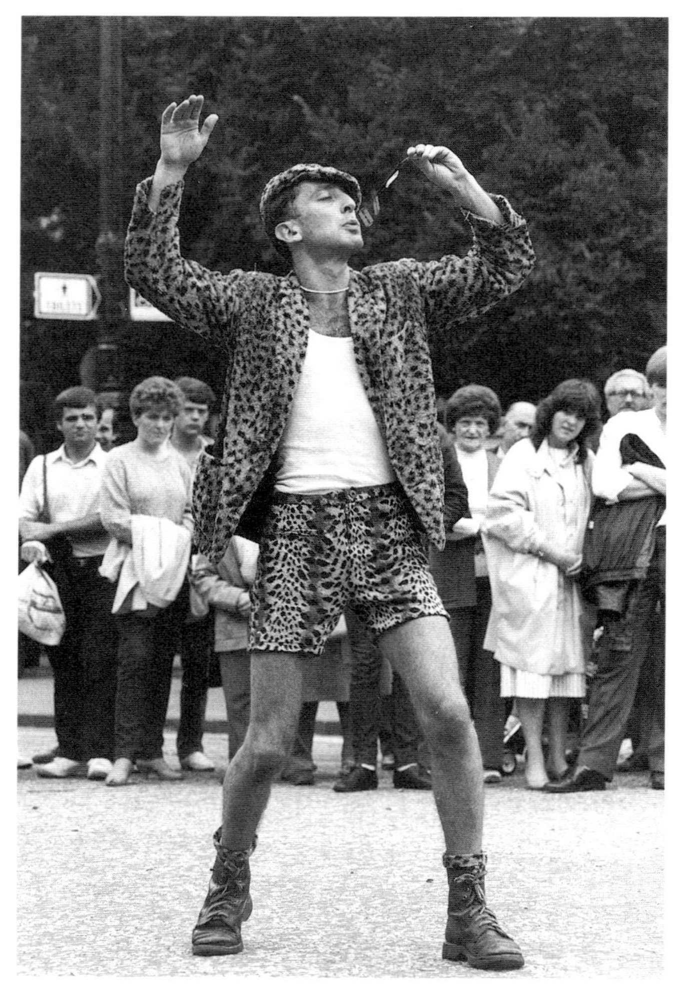

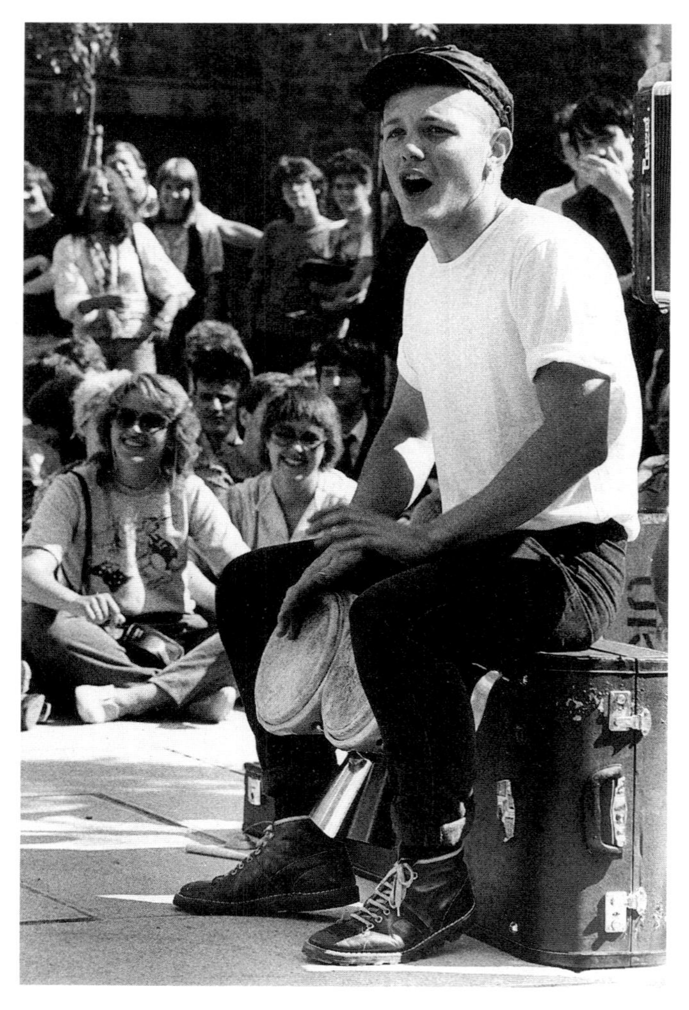

THE URBAN WARRIORS | 1985 | TOP LEFT

BILL McKENZIE | 1983 | TOP RIGHT

J J WALLER | 1983 | ABOVE LEFT

POOKIESNACKENBURGER | 1982 | ABOVE RIGHT

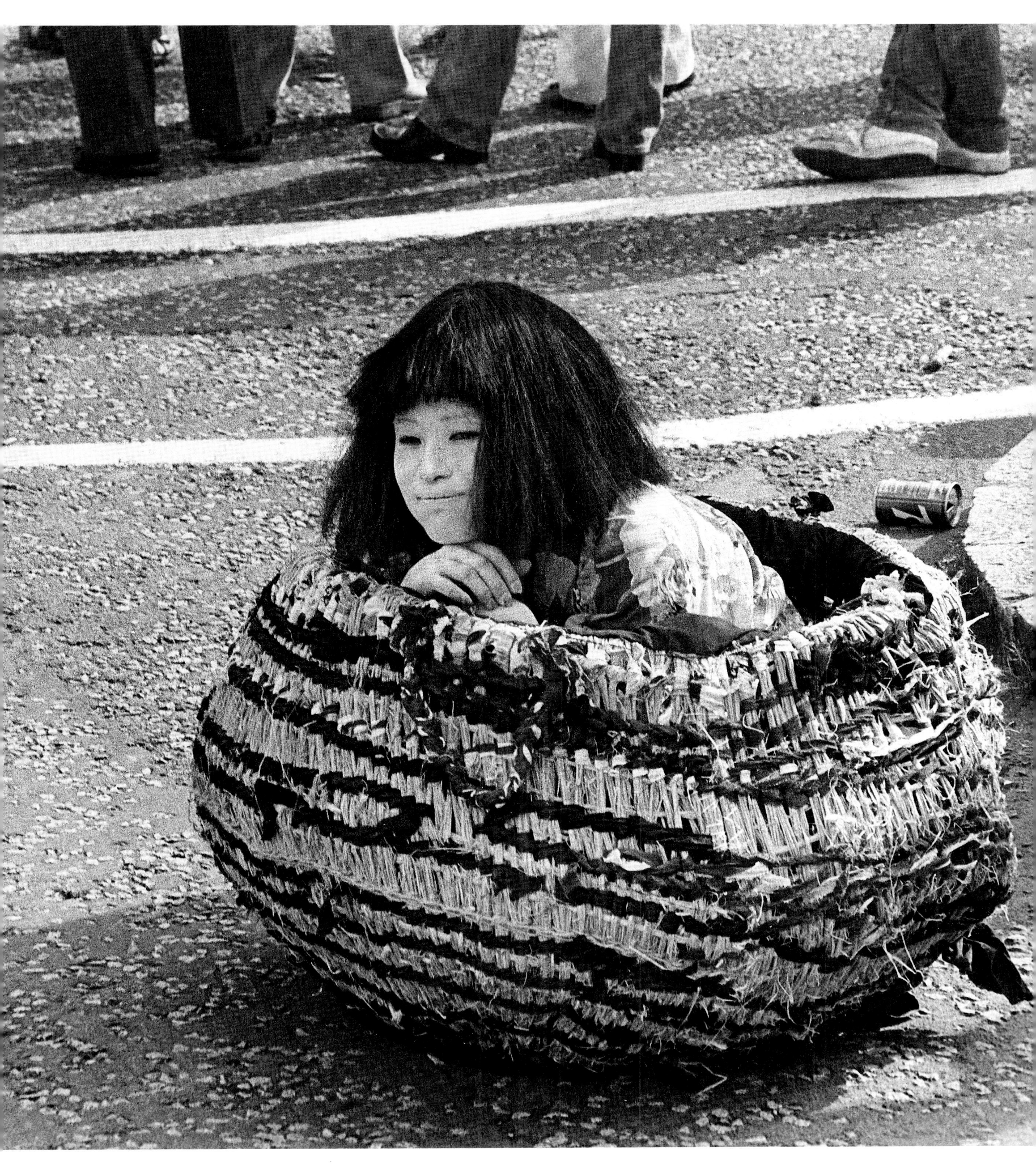

BHUTTO DANCE COMPANY | JAPAN | 1982

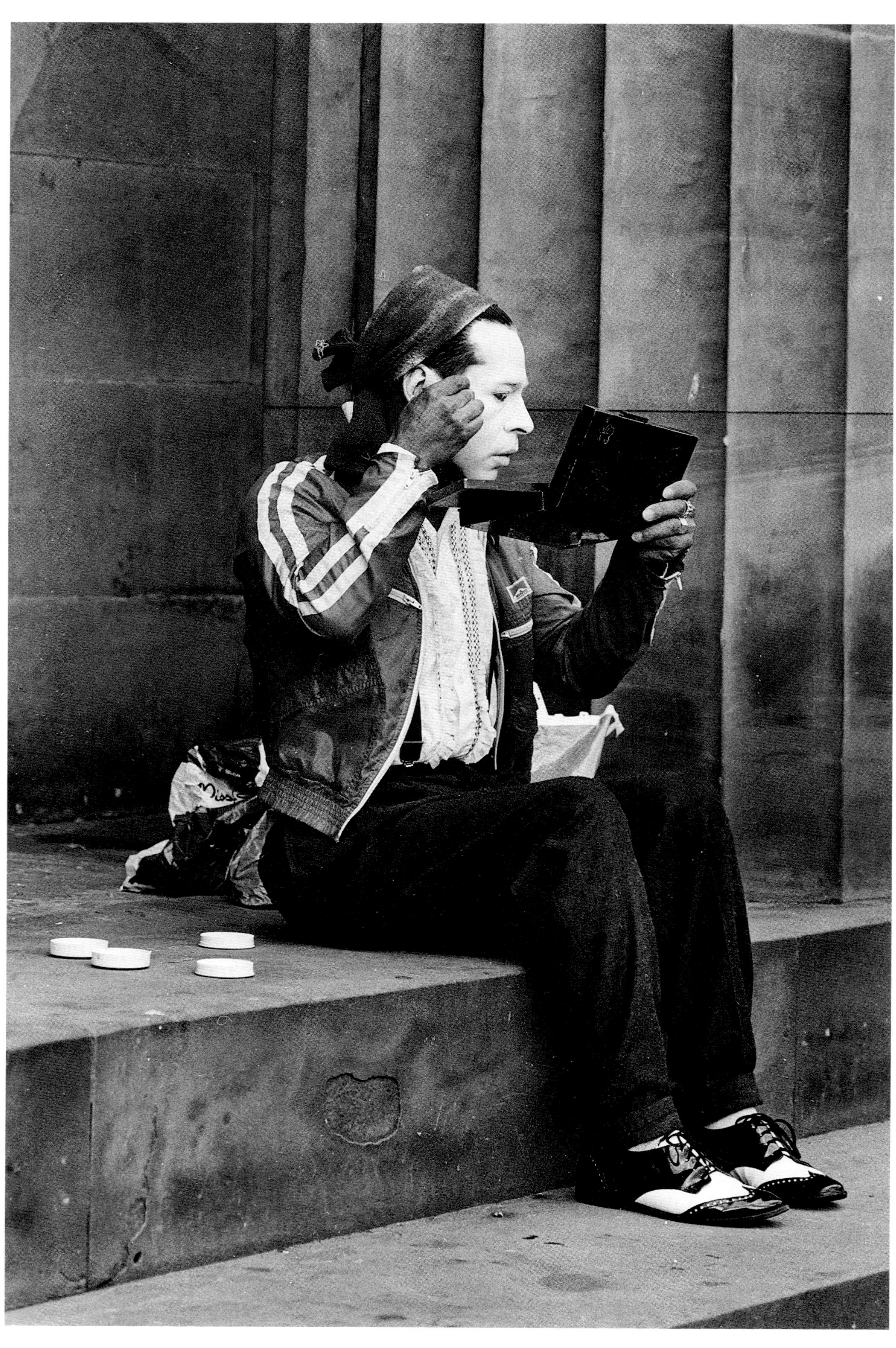

TOPO GRAJEDA | 1985

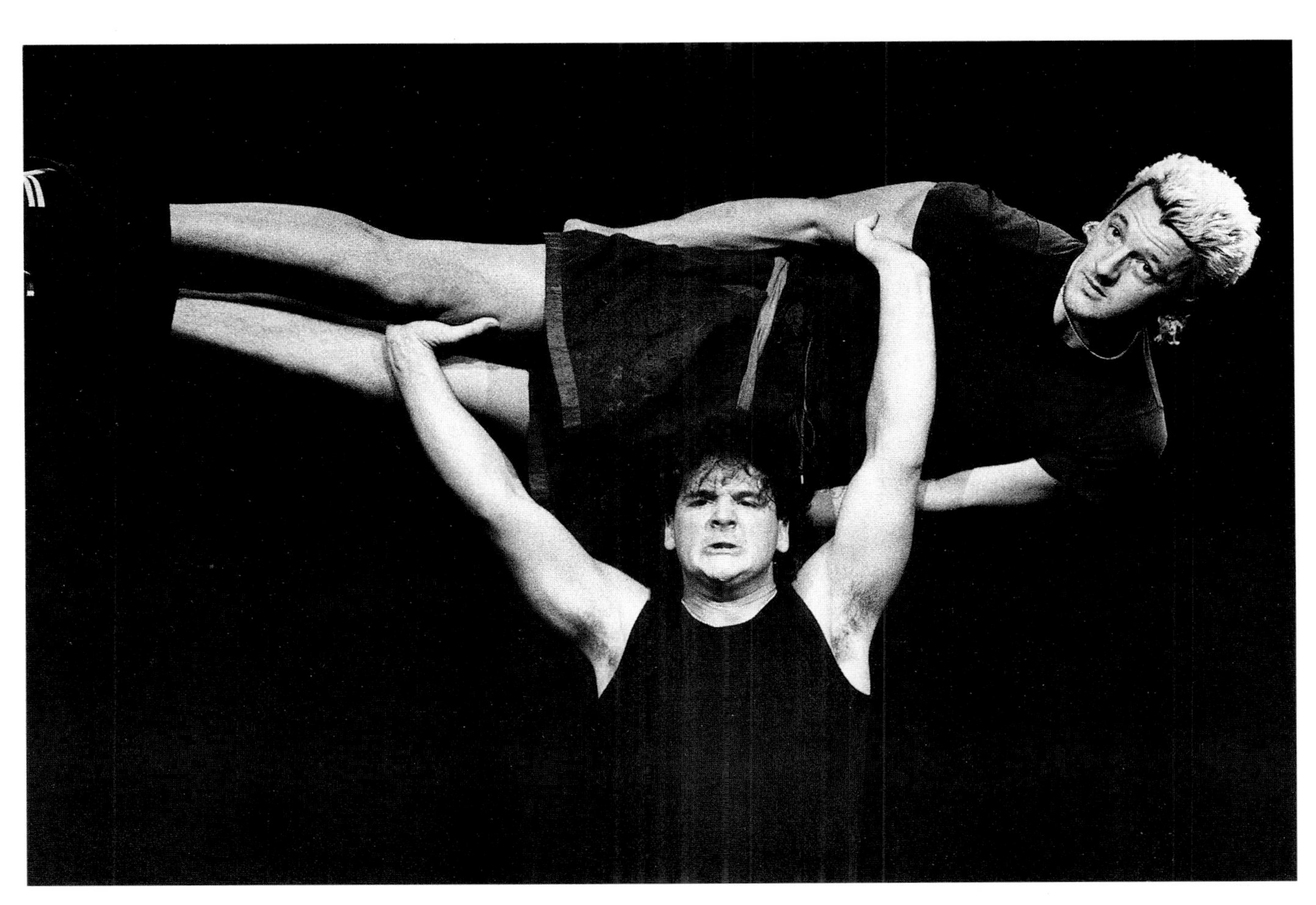

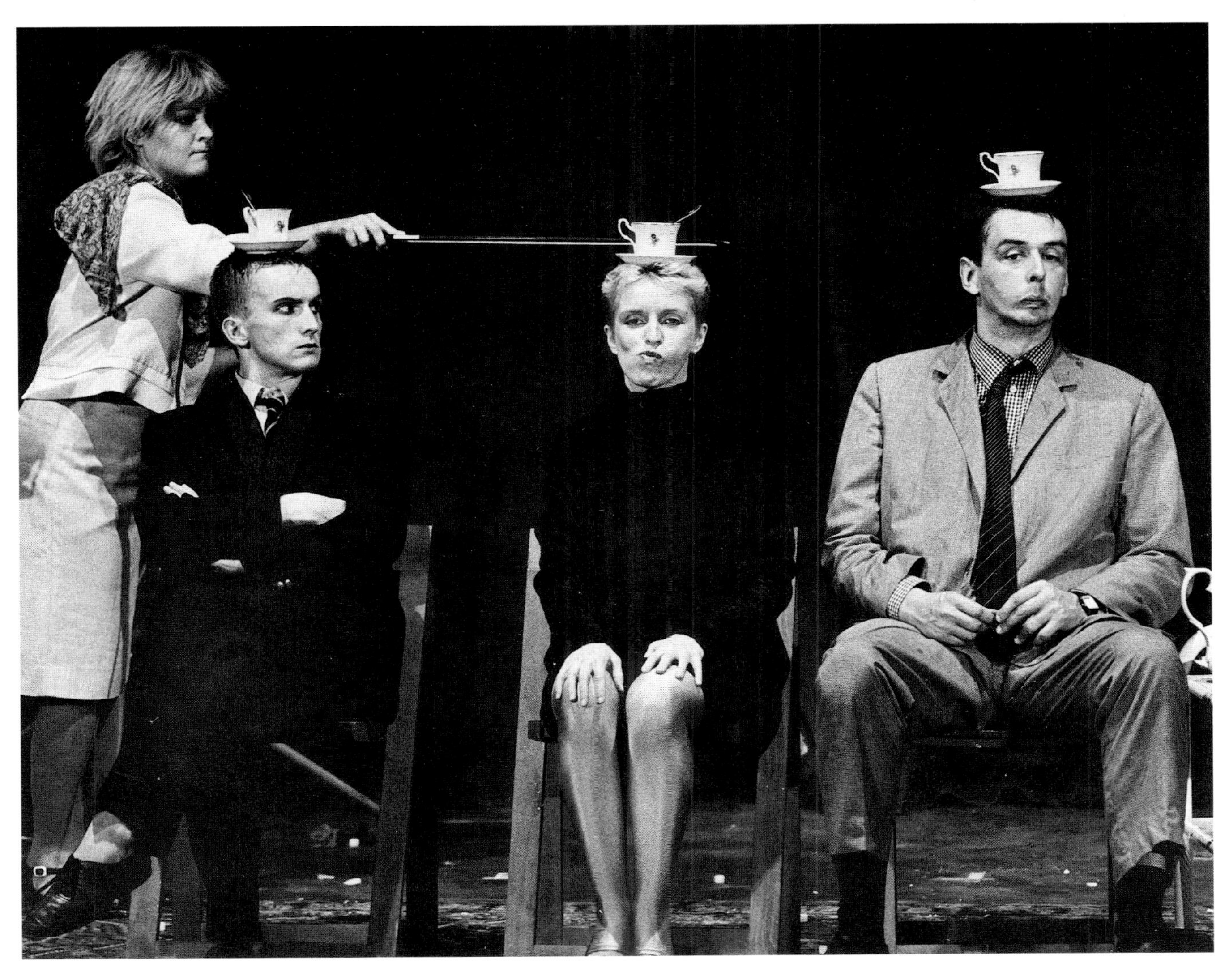

THE VIC OUS BOYS | ASSEMBLY ROOMS | 1986 | TOP

RA RA ZOO | ELEPHANT TENT | 1986

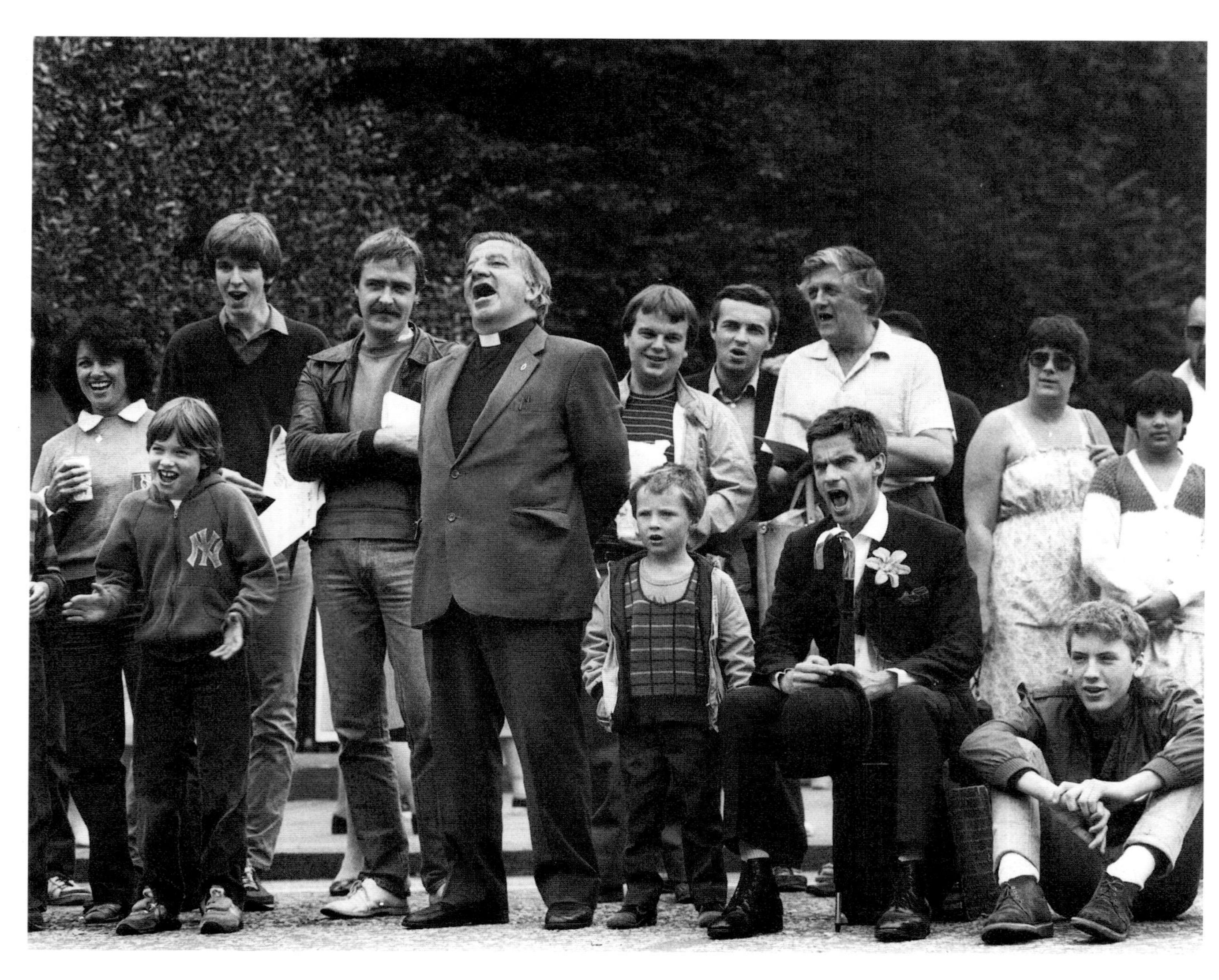

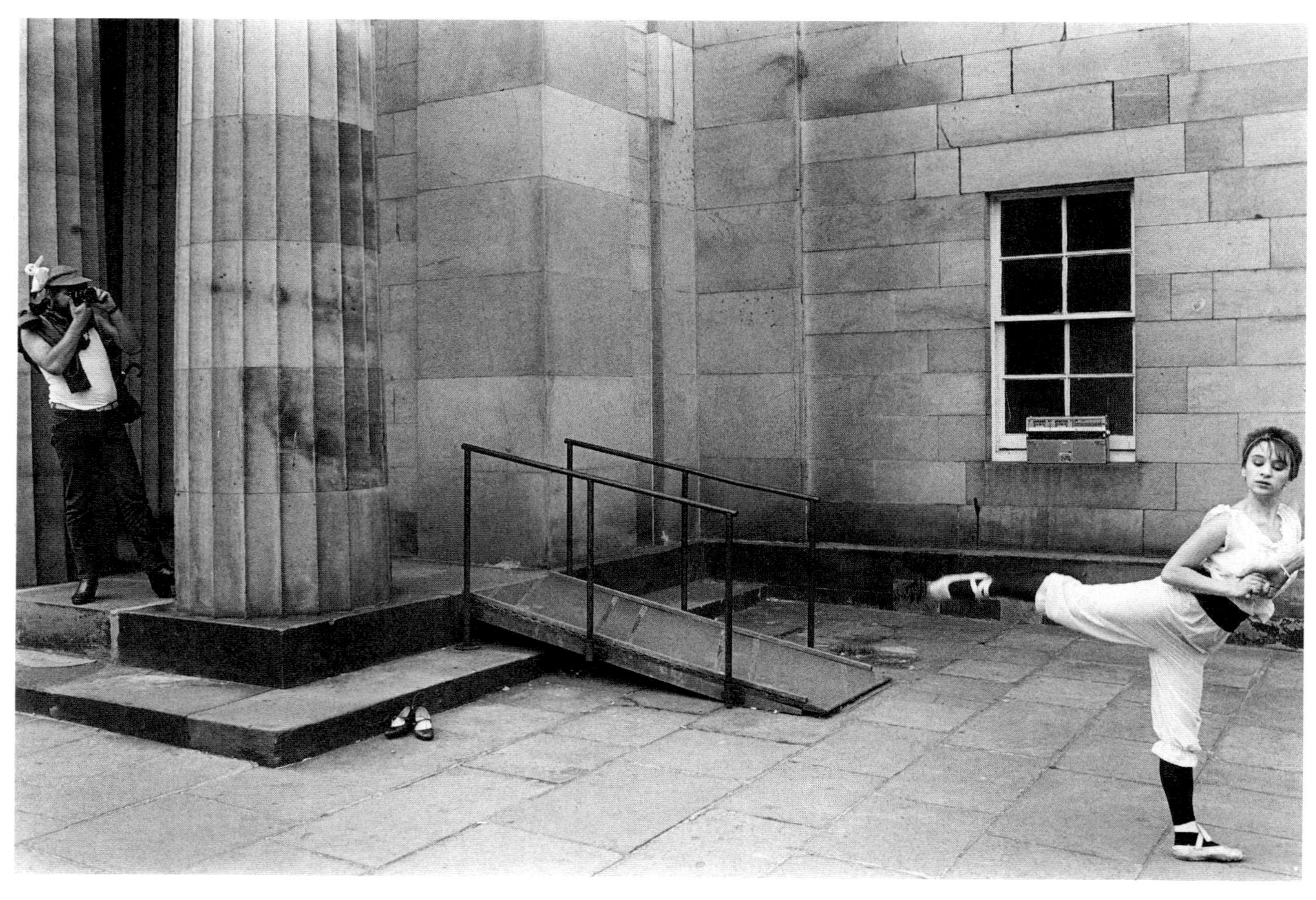

AUDIENCE PARTICIPATION | THE MOUND | 1983 | TOP

DANCING SHOES | THE MOUND | 1983

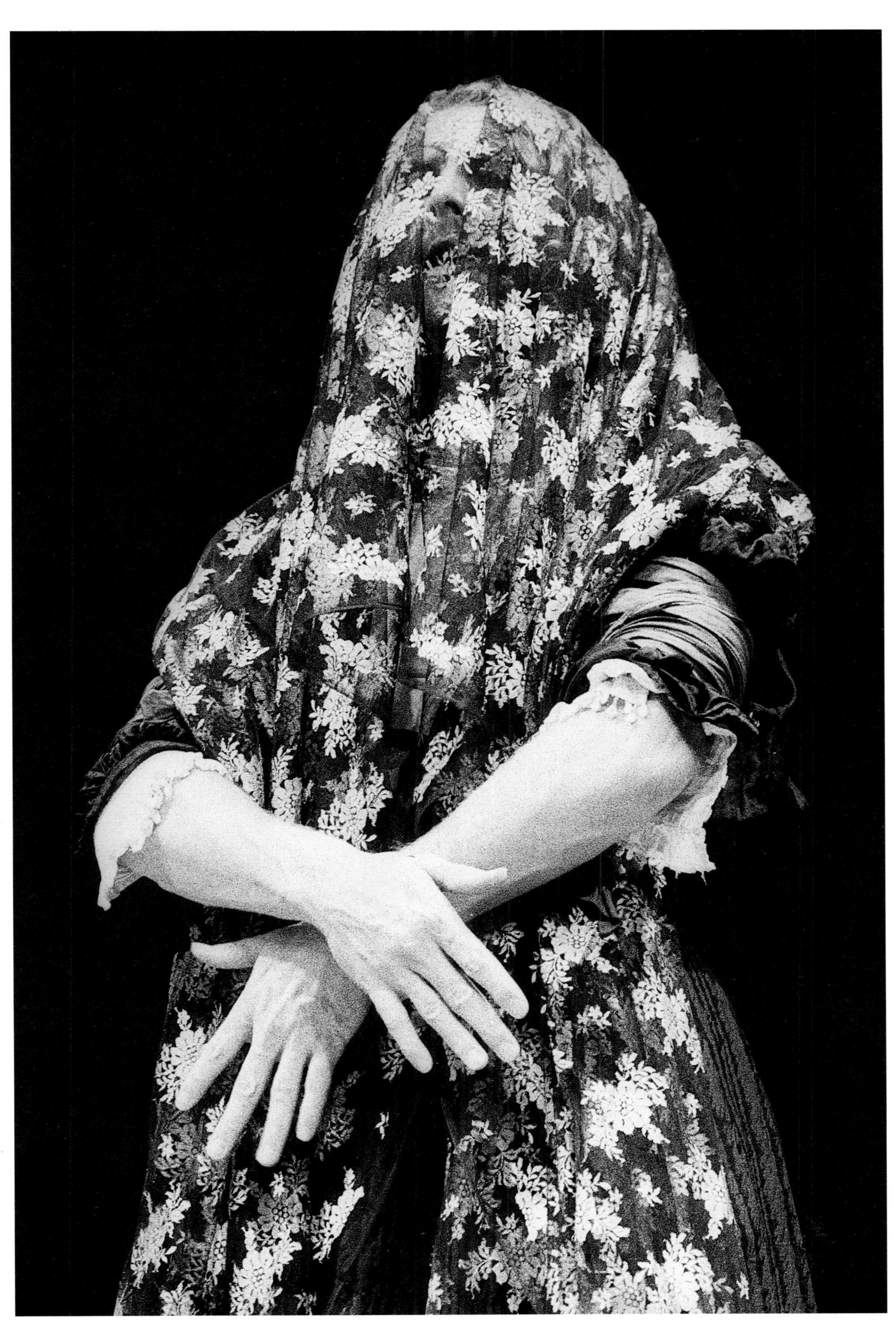

'HAMLET' | OXFORD PLAYERS | 1986

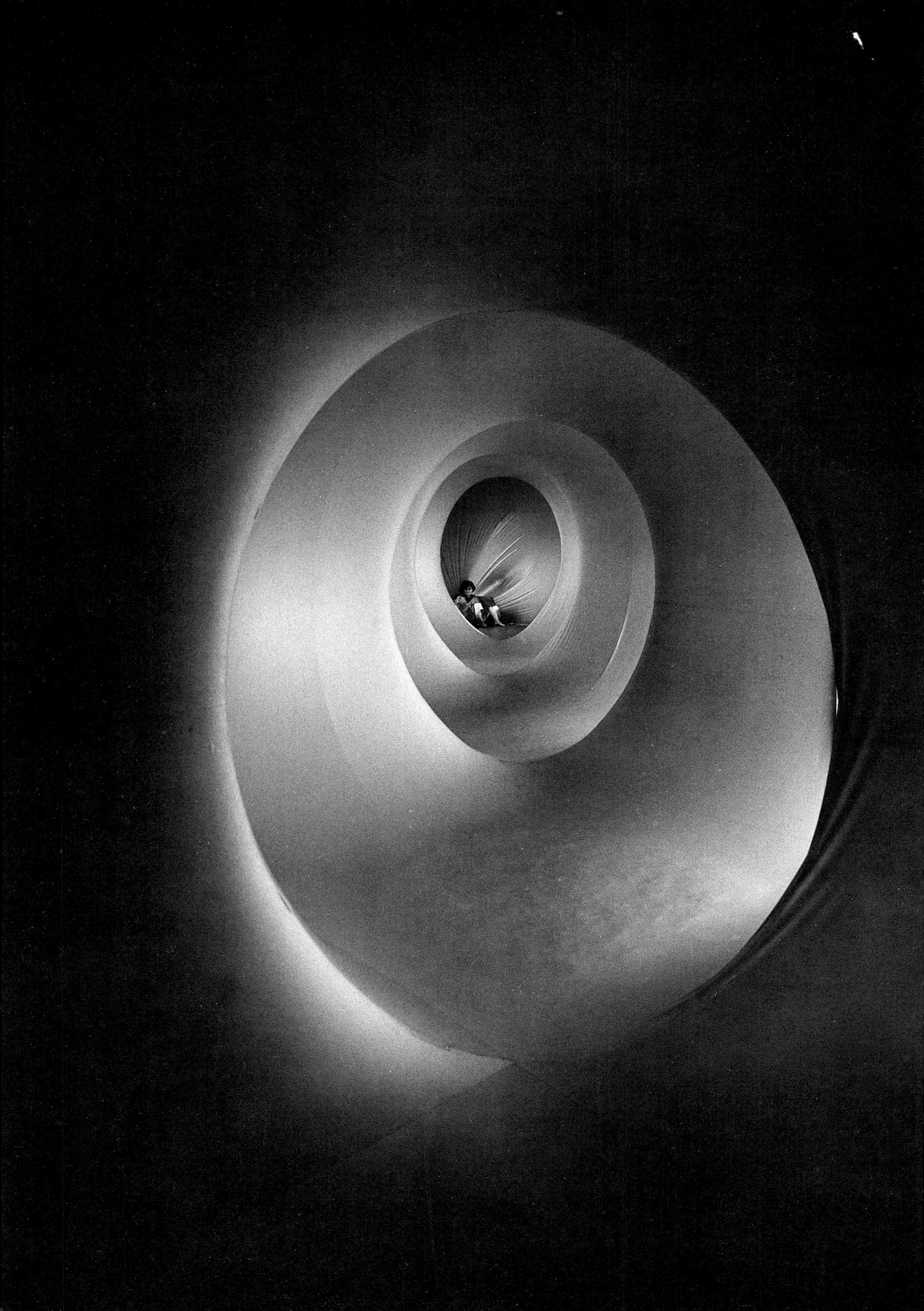

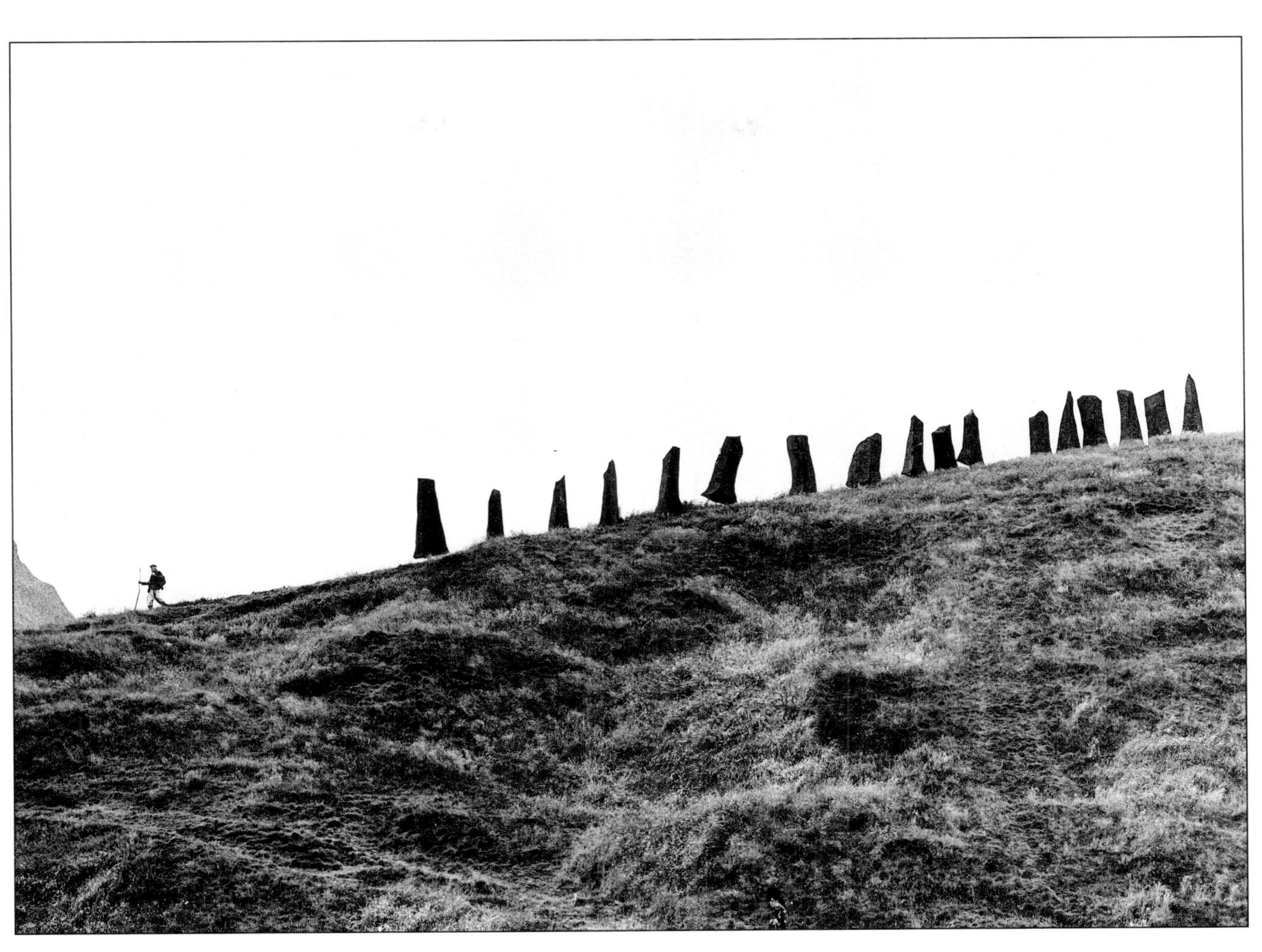

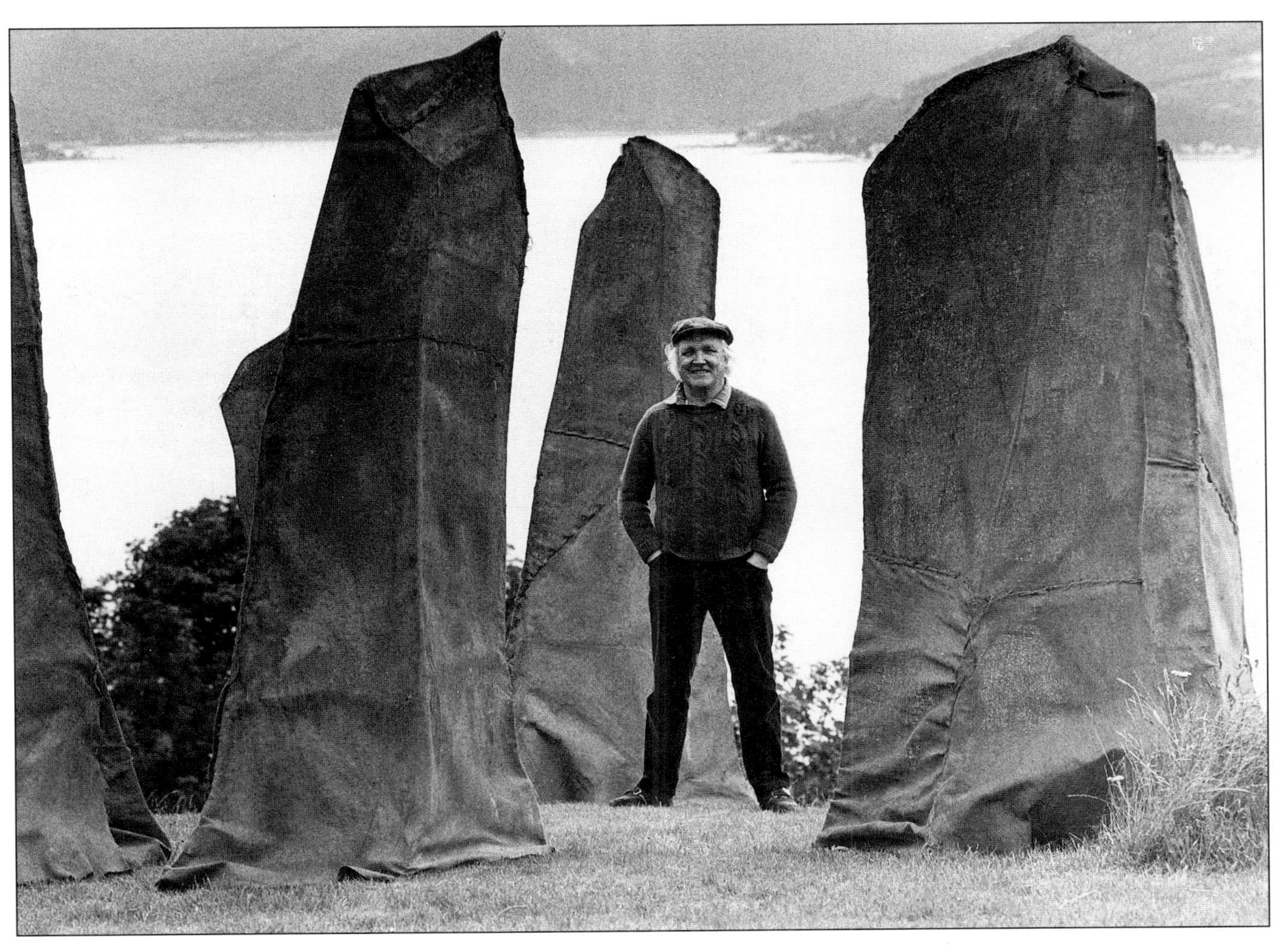

'COLOURSCAPE' | PRINCES STREET GARDENS | 1985 | OPPOSITE

THE ARRIVAL OF GEORGE WYLLIE AND THE STONES OF MUCKLE CHUCKLE | TOP | AFTER THE LONG MARCH FROM GOUROCK | ABOVE | 1985

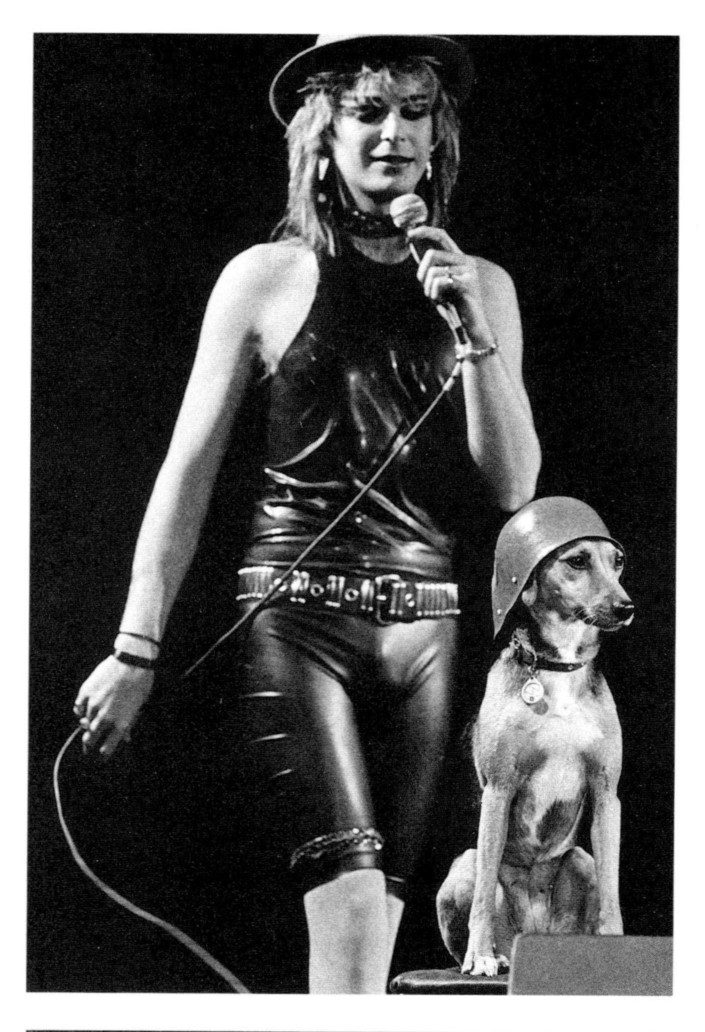

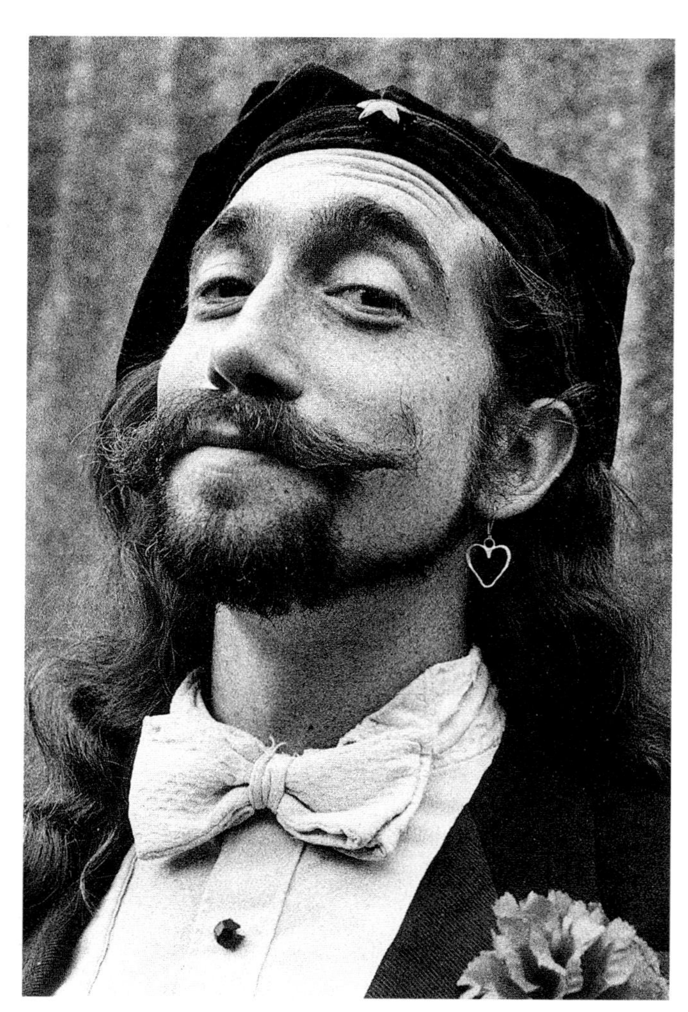

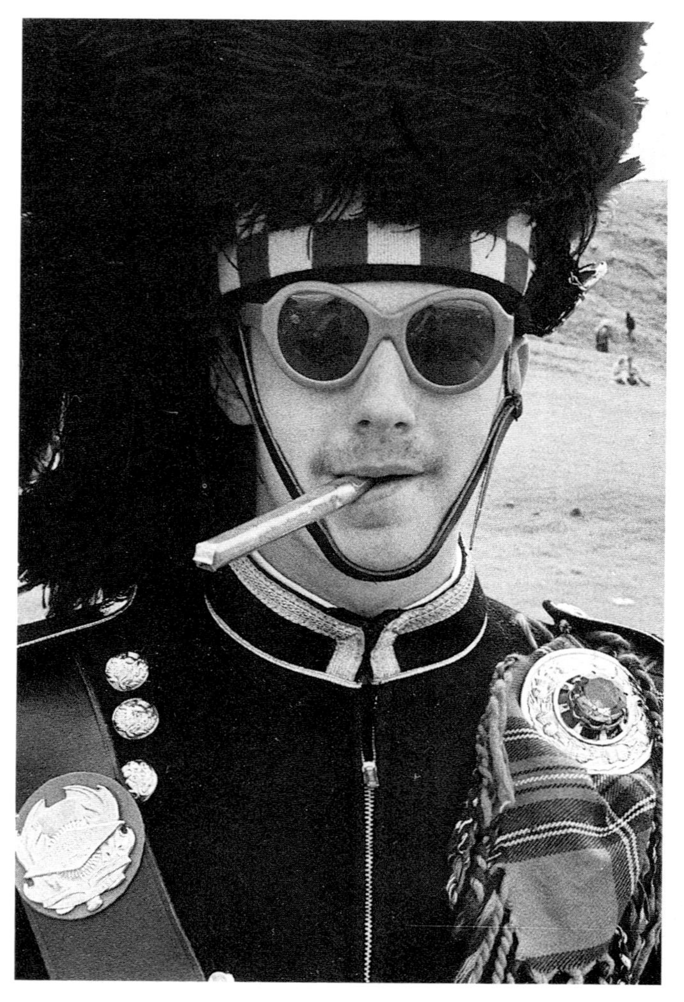

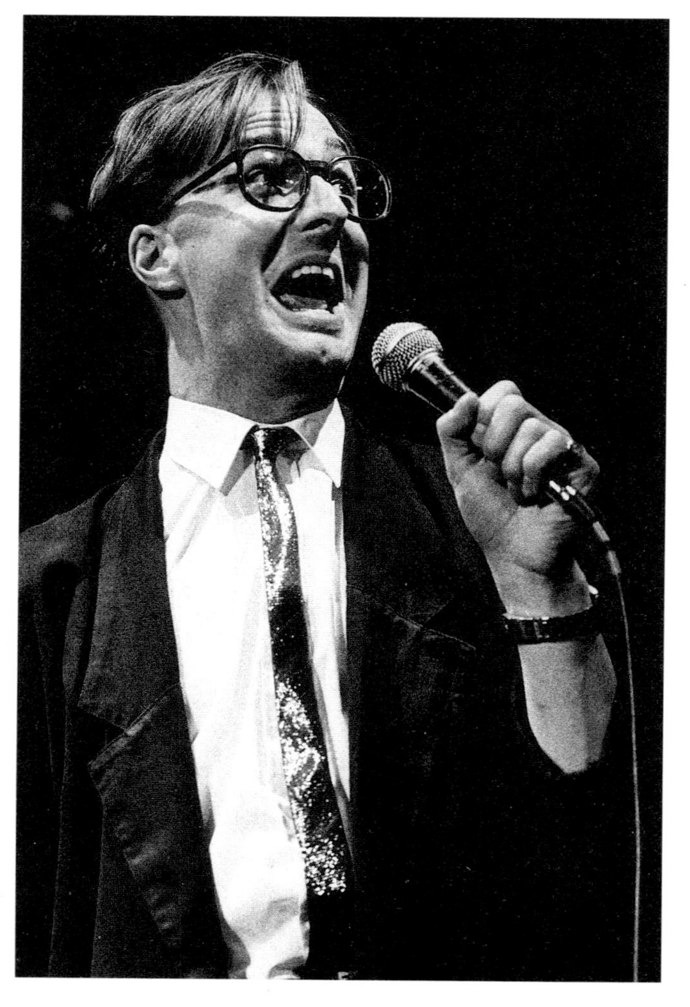

JOAN COLLINS FAN CLUB | 1986 | TOP LEFT

IVAN KARAMAZOV | 1985 | TOP RIGHT

SOUTH QUEENSFERRY PIPER | 1986 | ABOVE LEFT

SIMON FANSHAW | 1986 | ABOVE RIGHT

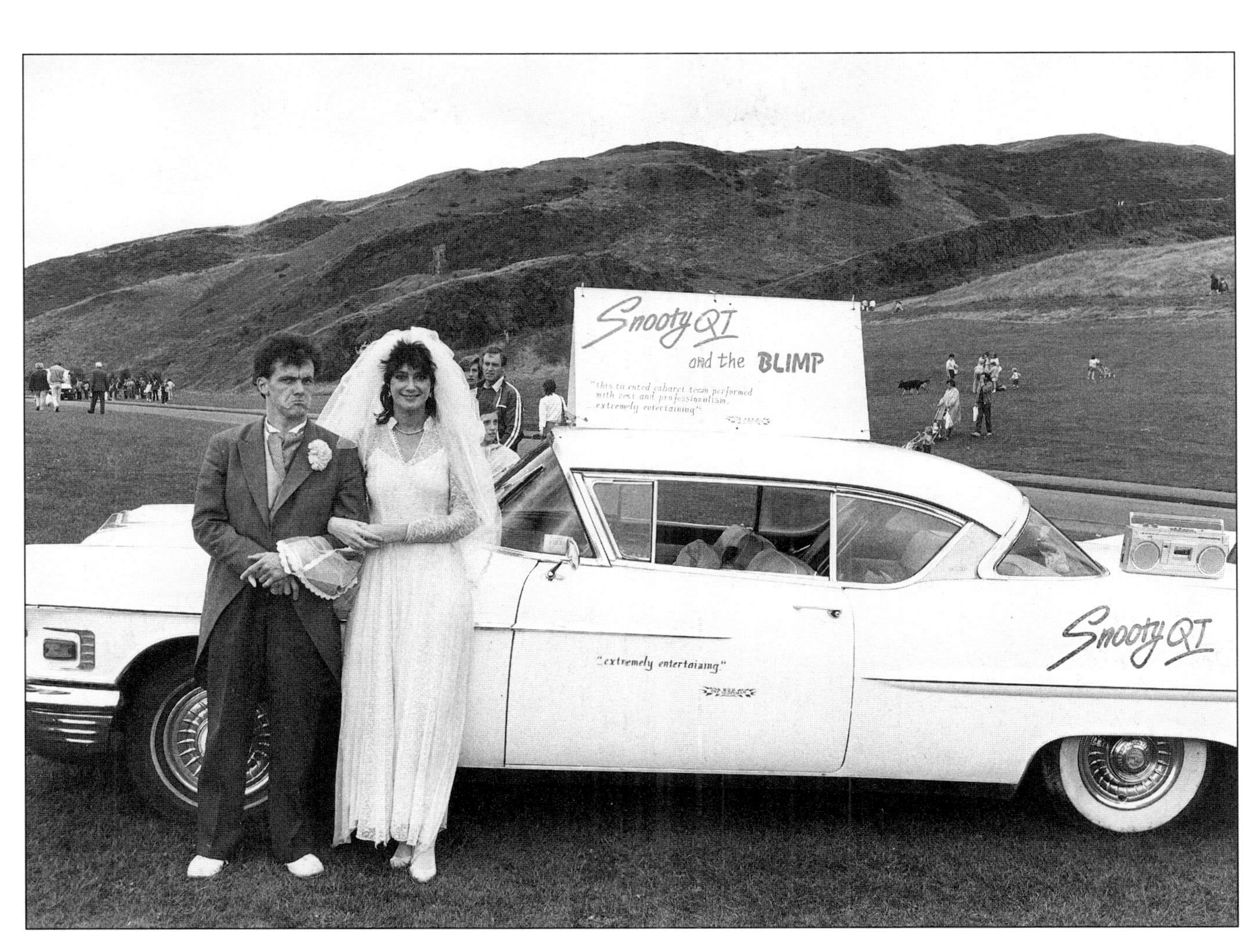

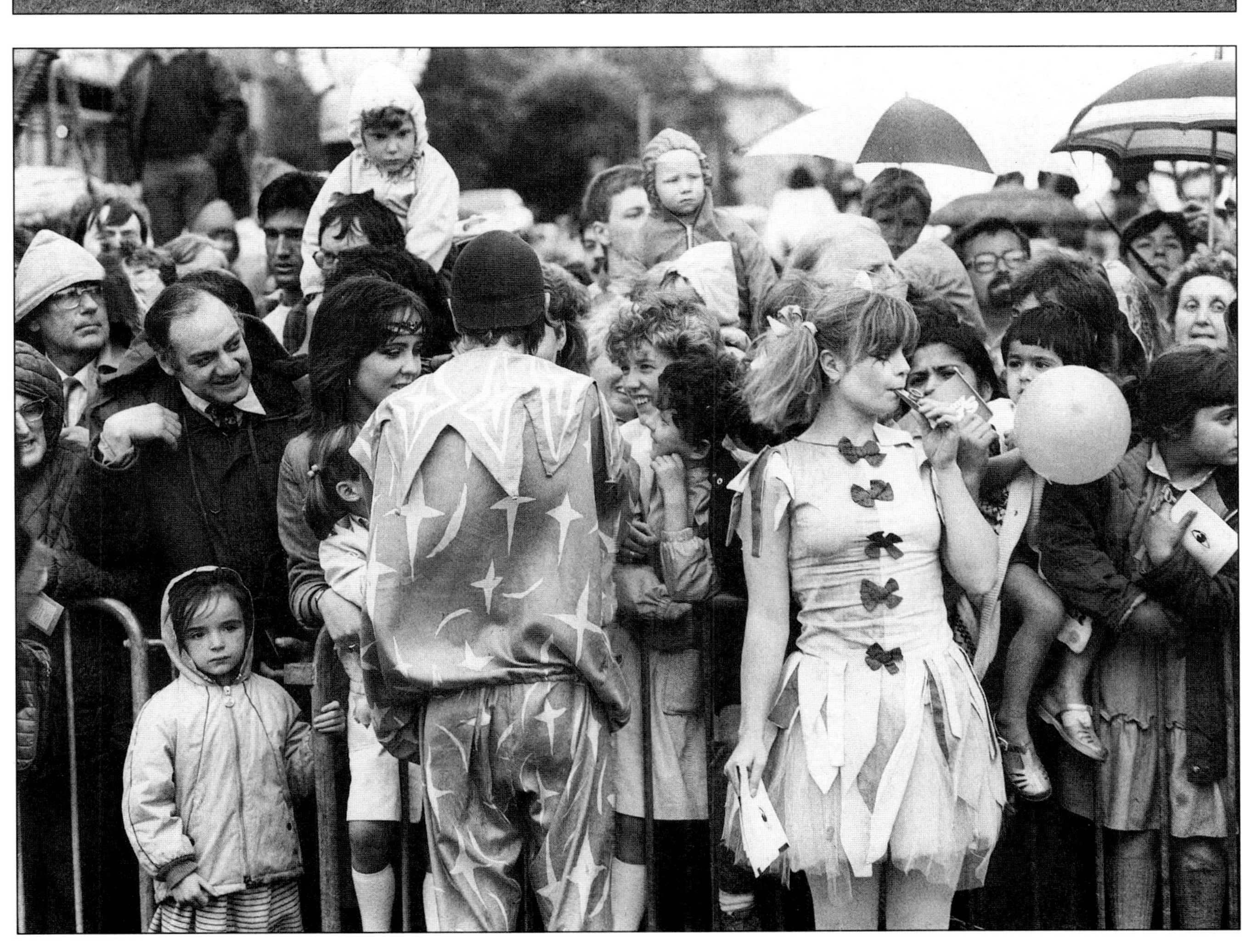

SNOOTY QT AND THE BLIMP | FRINGE SUNDAY | 1985

THE FOOL'S TOYBOX | OPENING PARADE | 1985

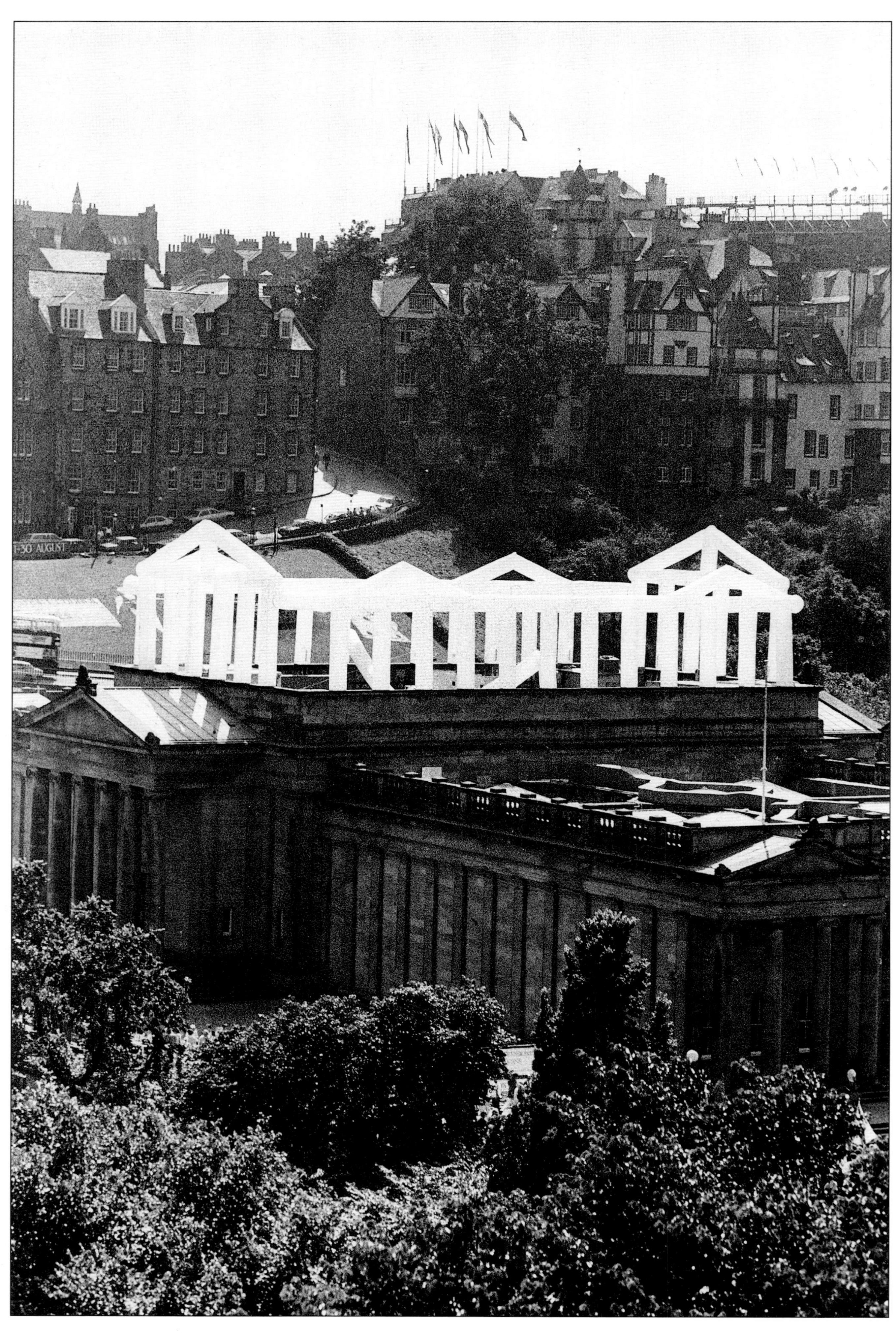
-30 AUGUST

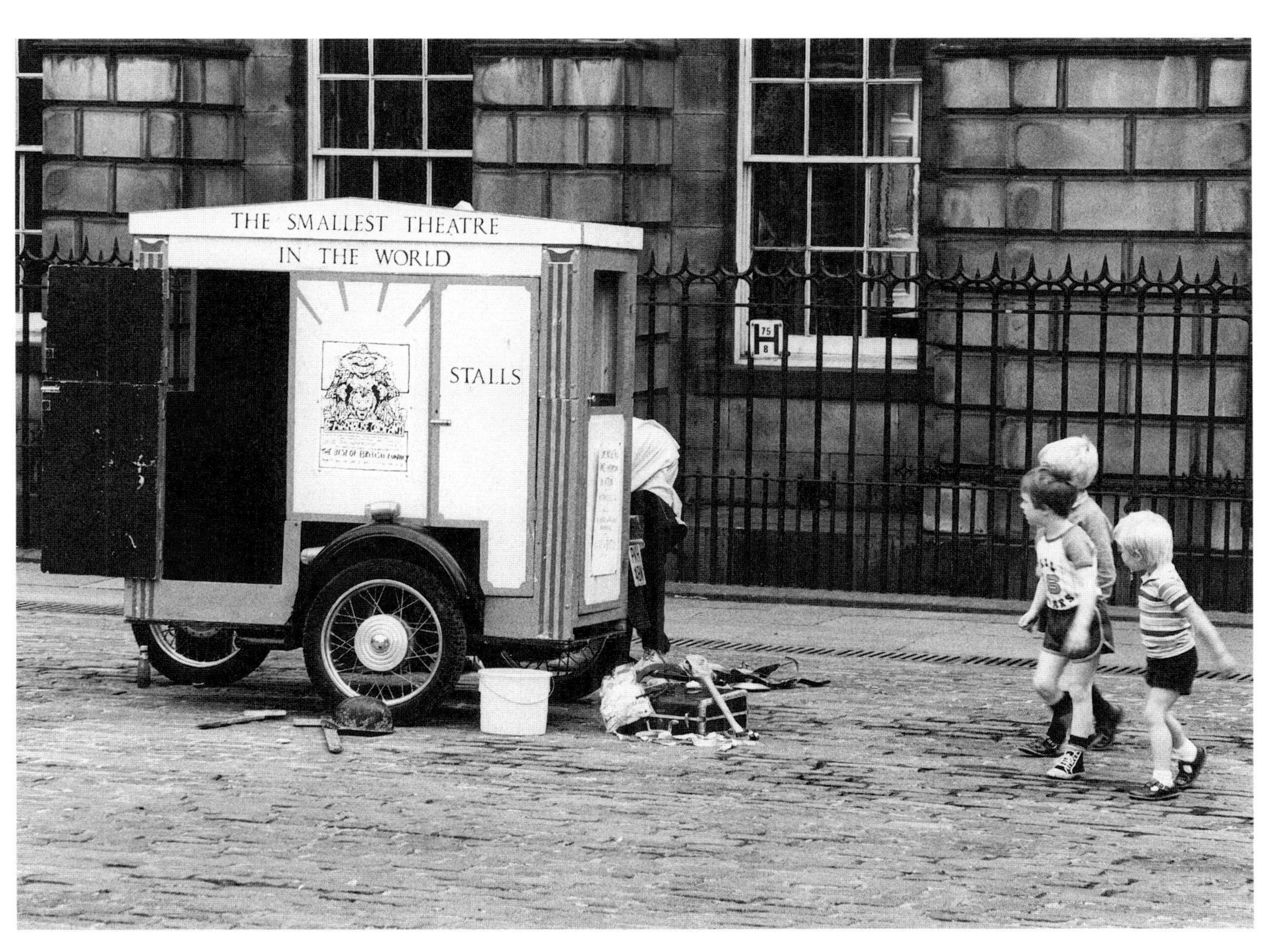

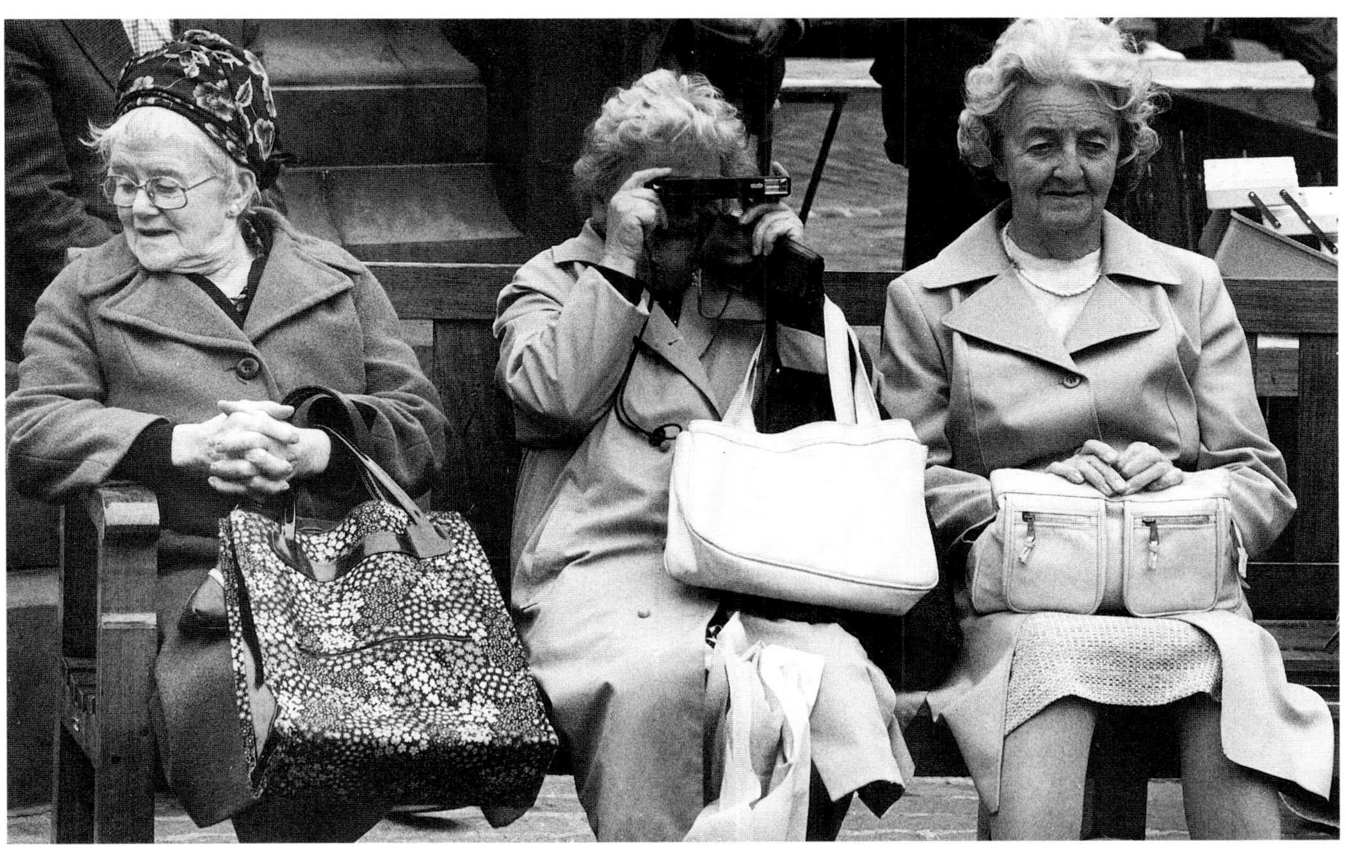

THE SMALLEST THEATRE IN THE WORLD | 1982

PARLIAMENT SQUARE | 1982

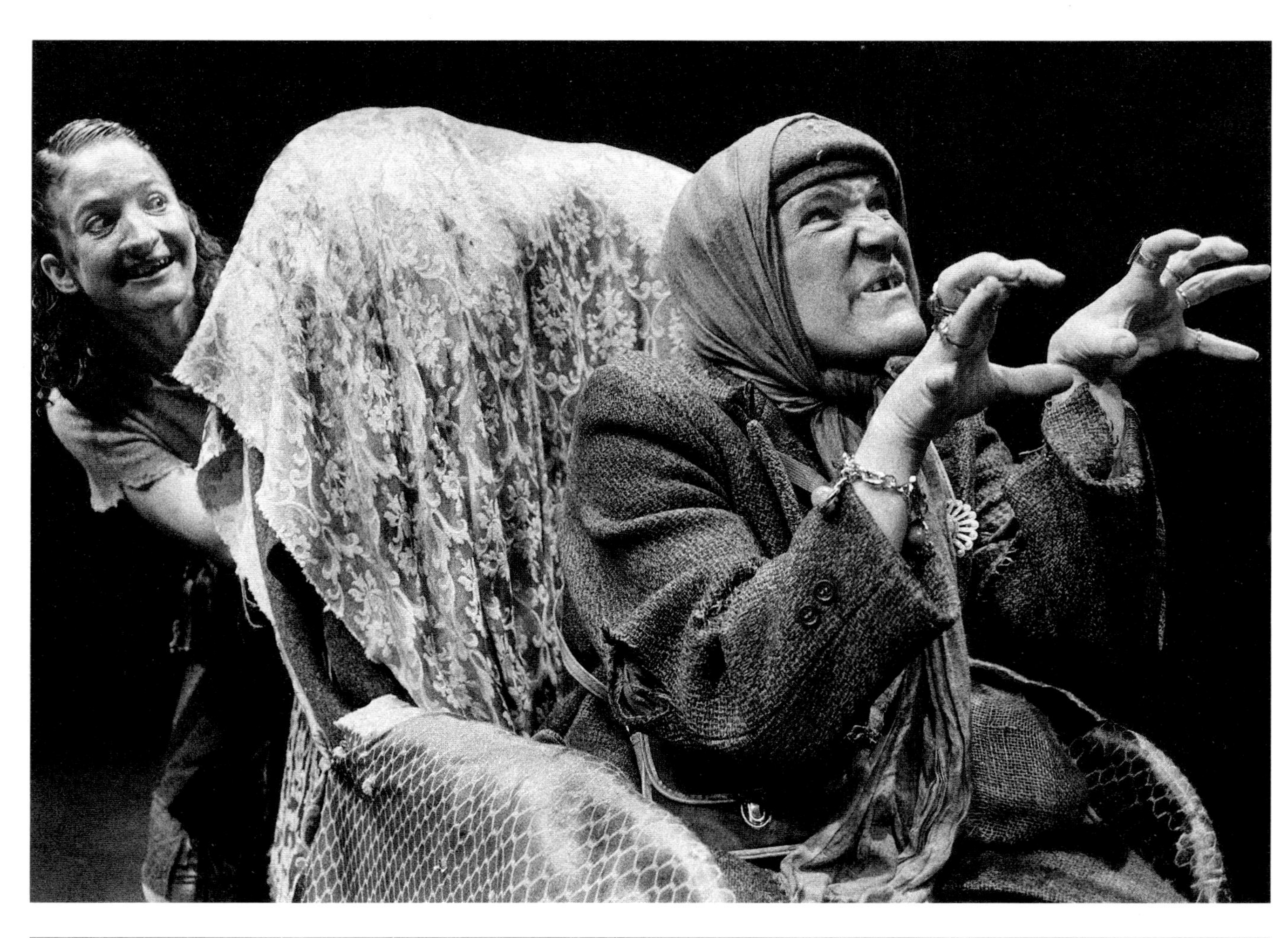

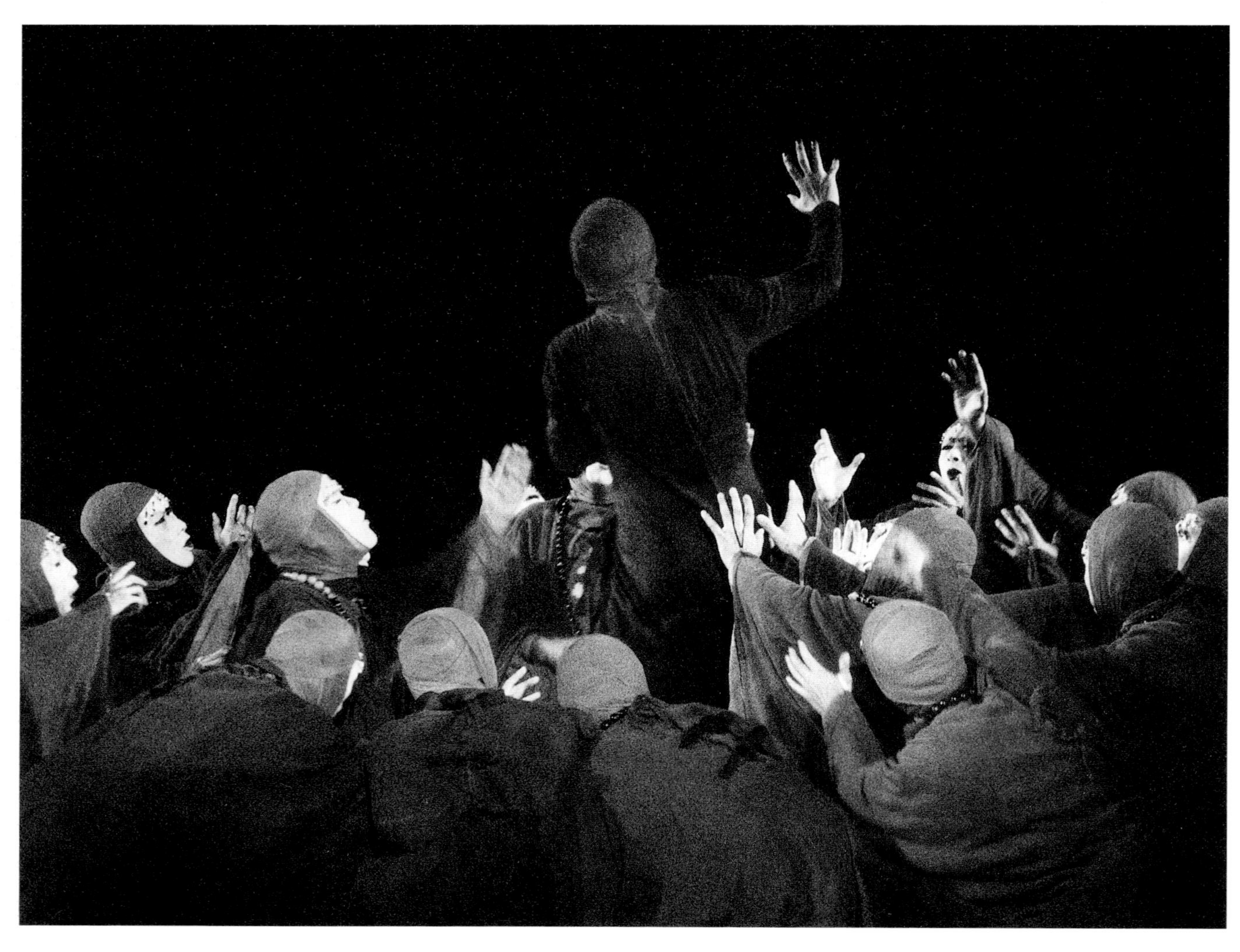

COMPAGNIE PHILIPPE GAULIER | TRAVERSE THEATRE | 1985 | TOP

'MEDEA' | TOHO COMPANY OF JAPAN | 1986

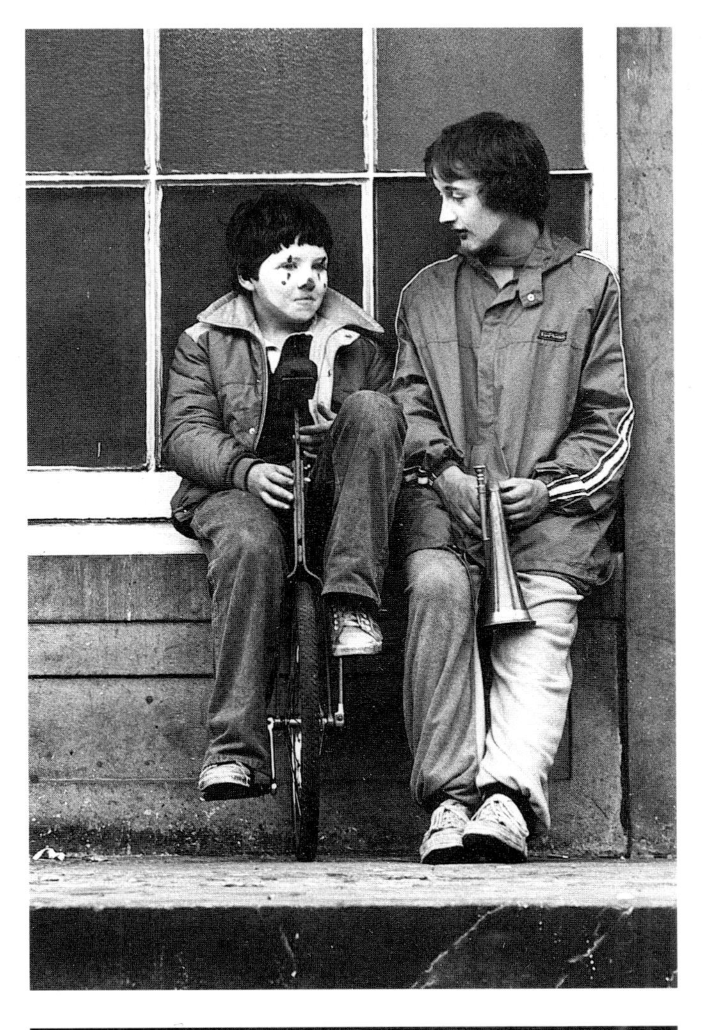

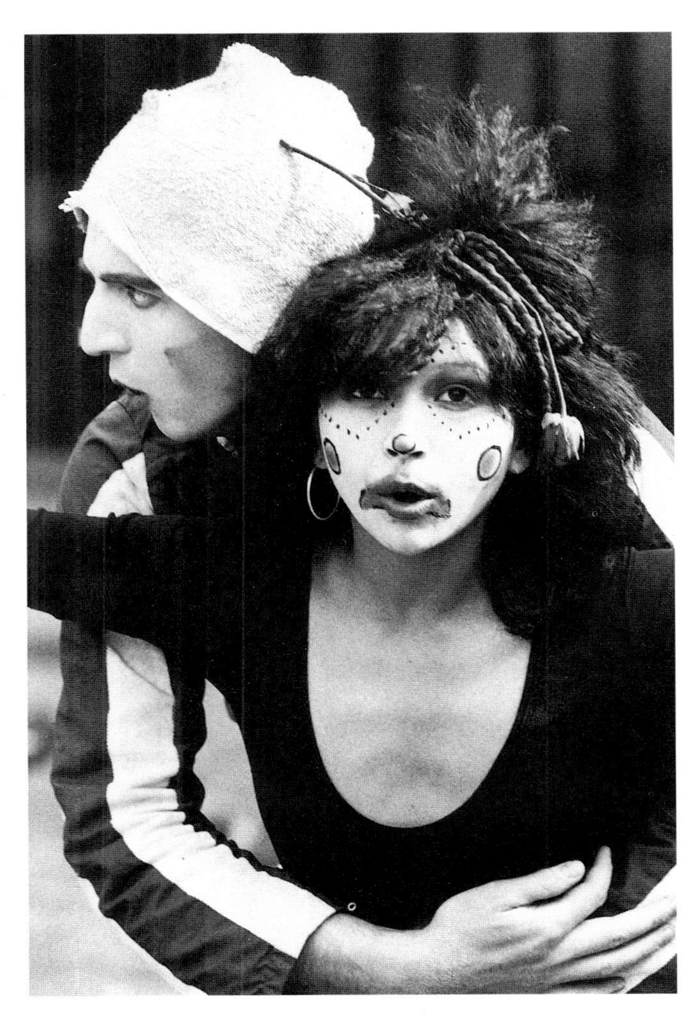

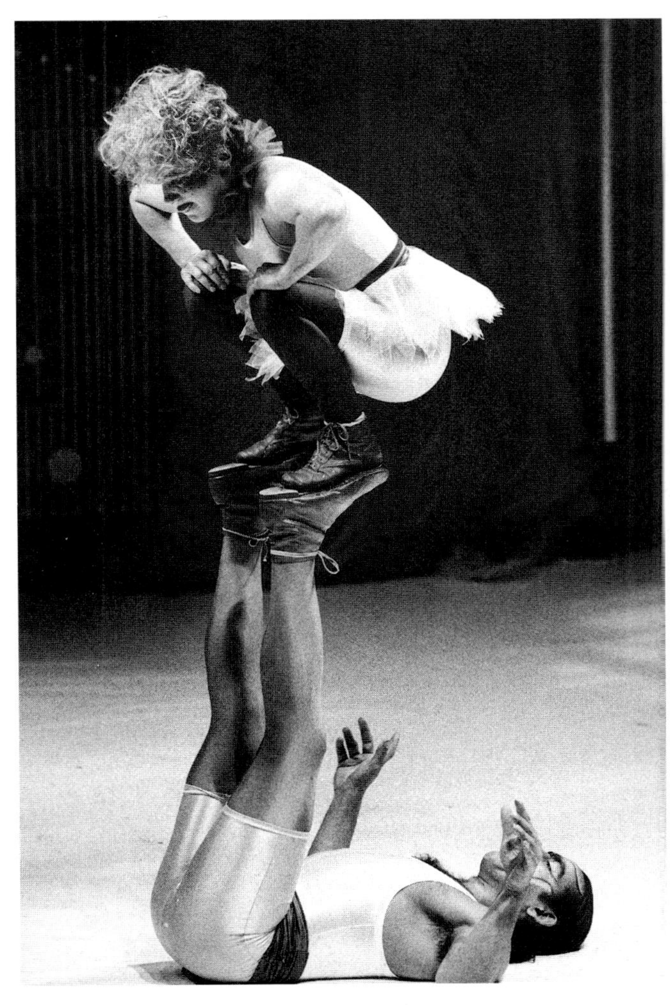

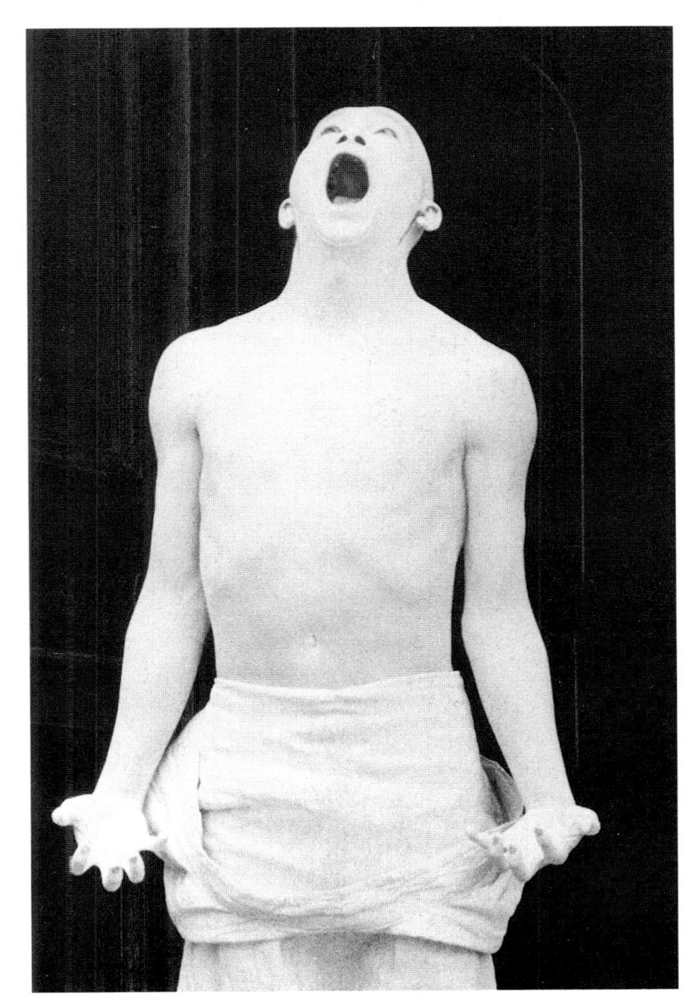

MEMBERS OF WESTER HAILES CHILDRENS CIRCUS | 1982 | TOP LEFT

STREET MIME | 1982 | TOP RIGHT

CIRCUS SENSO | 1986 | ABOVE LEFT

SANKAI JUKU | 1982 | ABOVE RIGHT

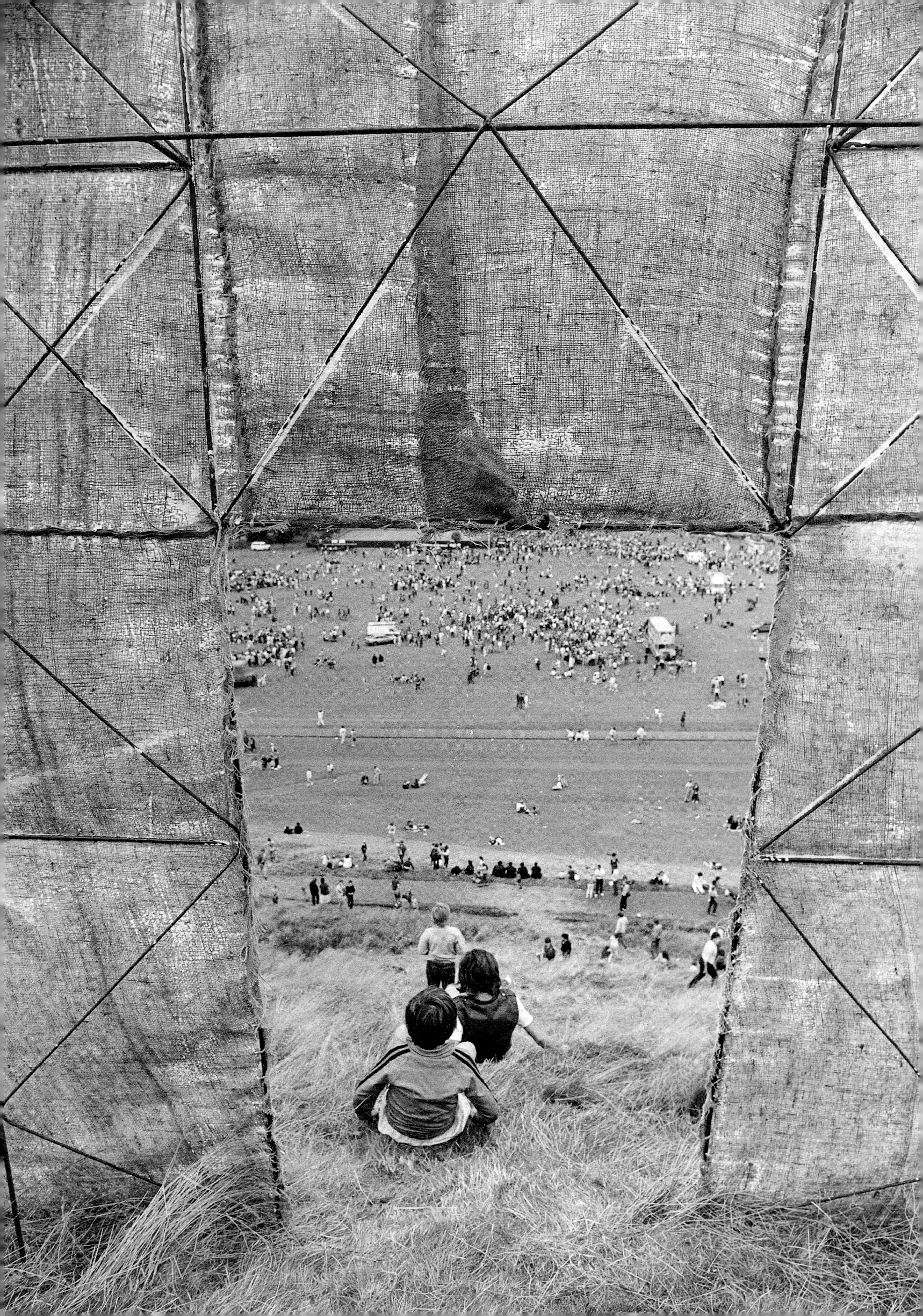

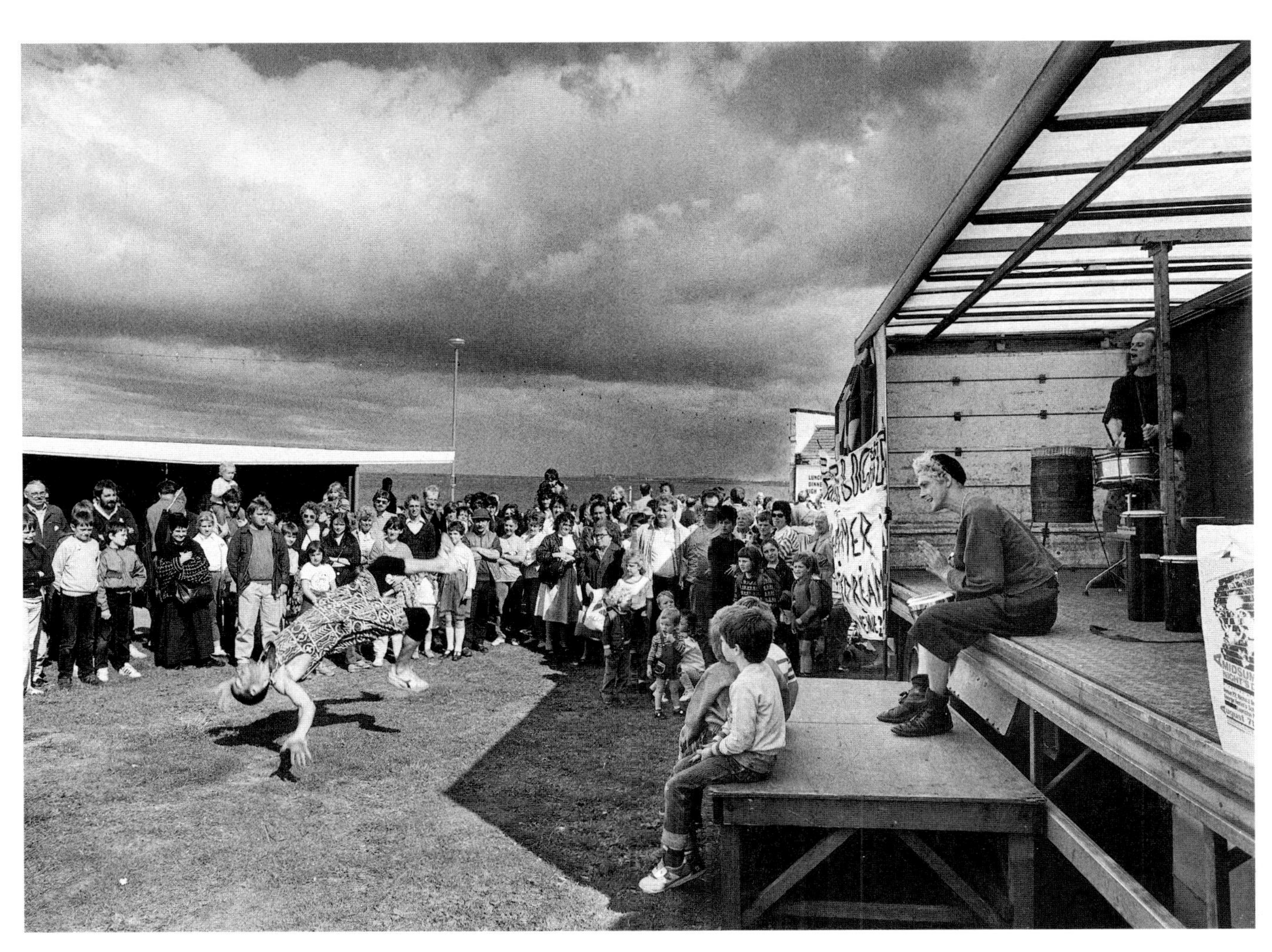

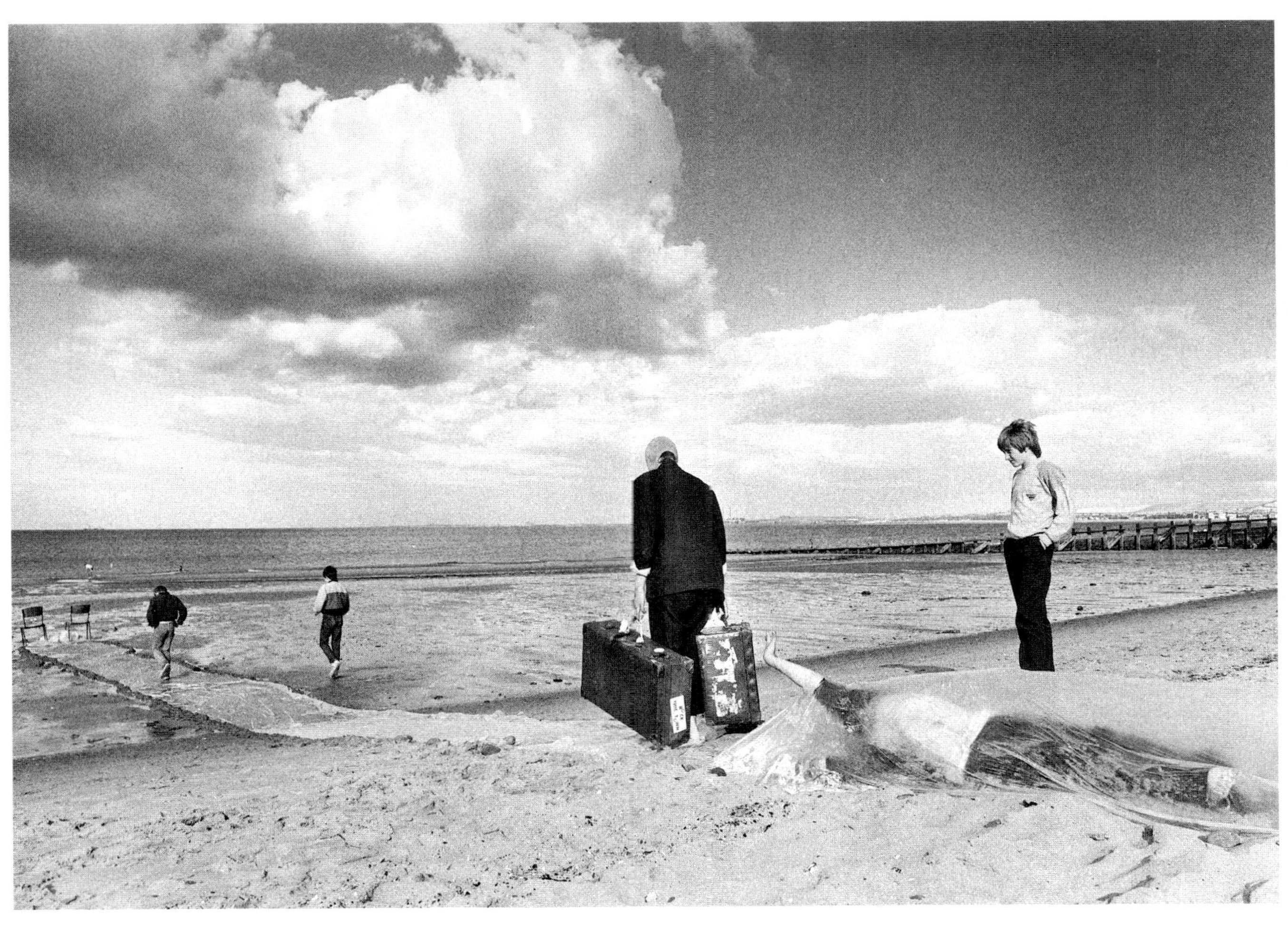

FRINGE SUNDAY | 1986 | OPPOSITE

FRINGE AT THE SEASIDE | PORTOBELLO | 1986 | TOP

ILLEGALARTS | PORTOBELLO | 1986

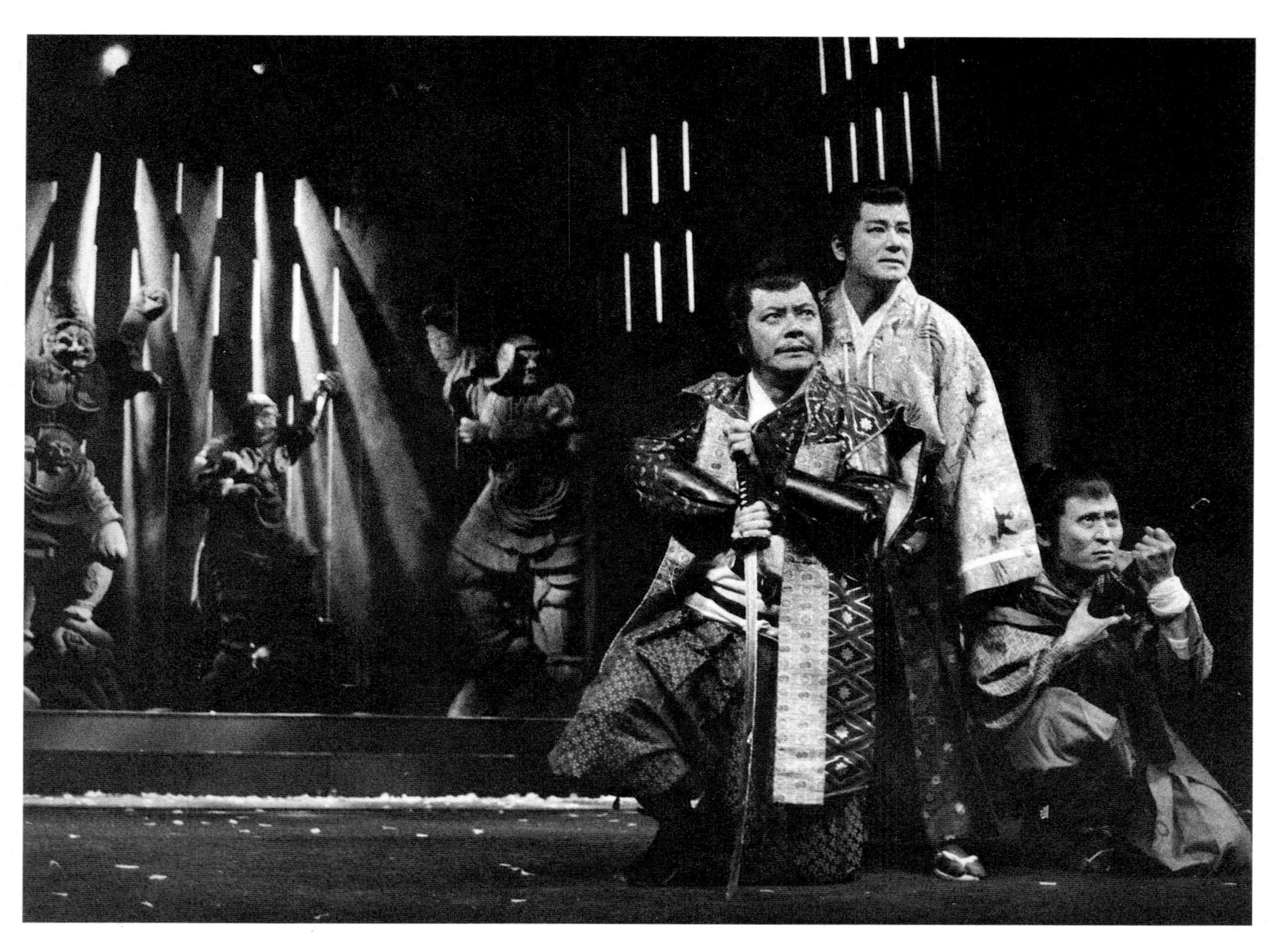

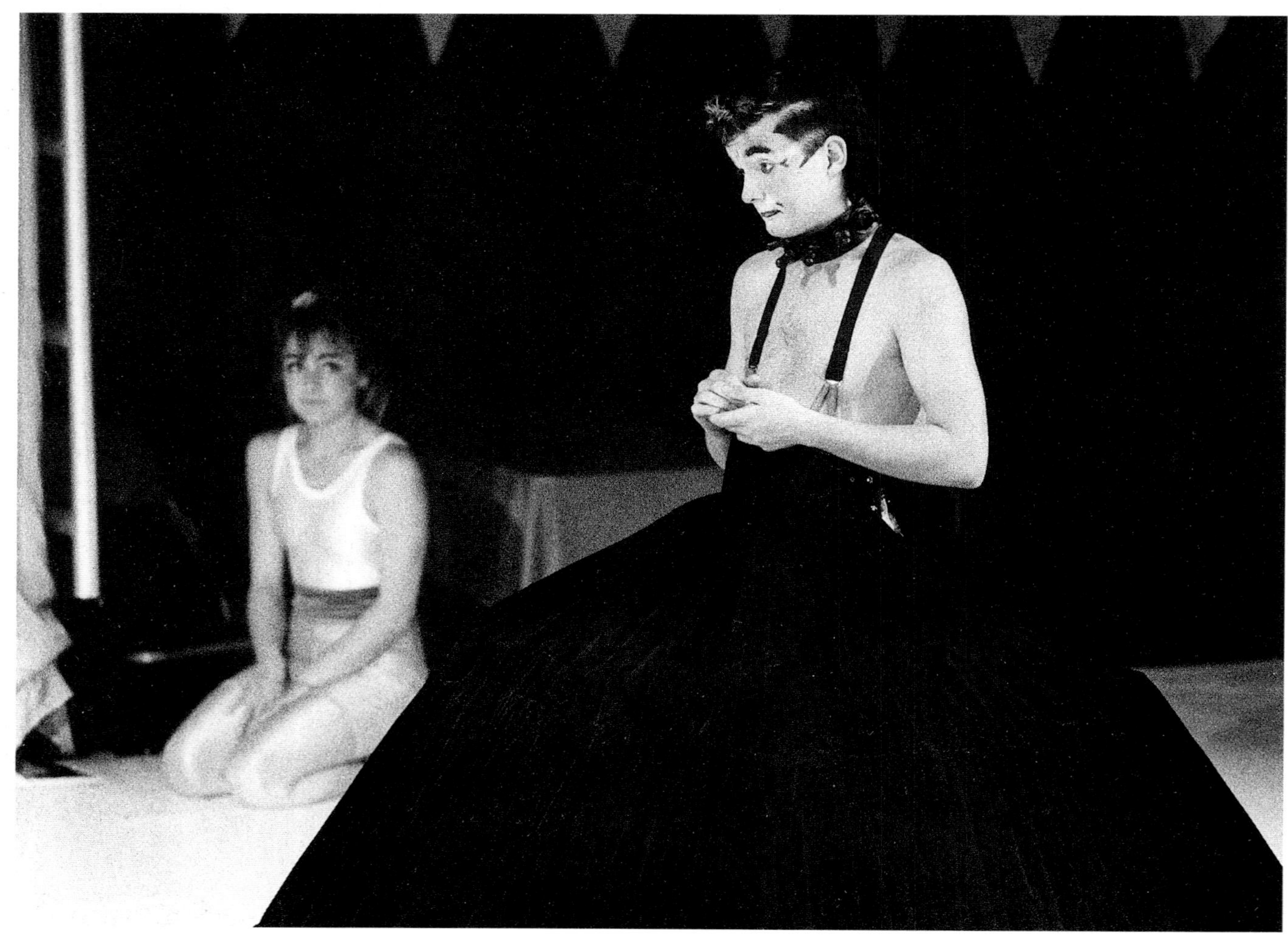

'MACBETH' | TOHO COMPANY OF JAPAN | 1985 | TOP

CIRCUS SENSO | 1986

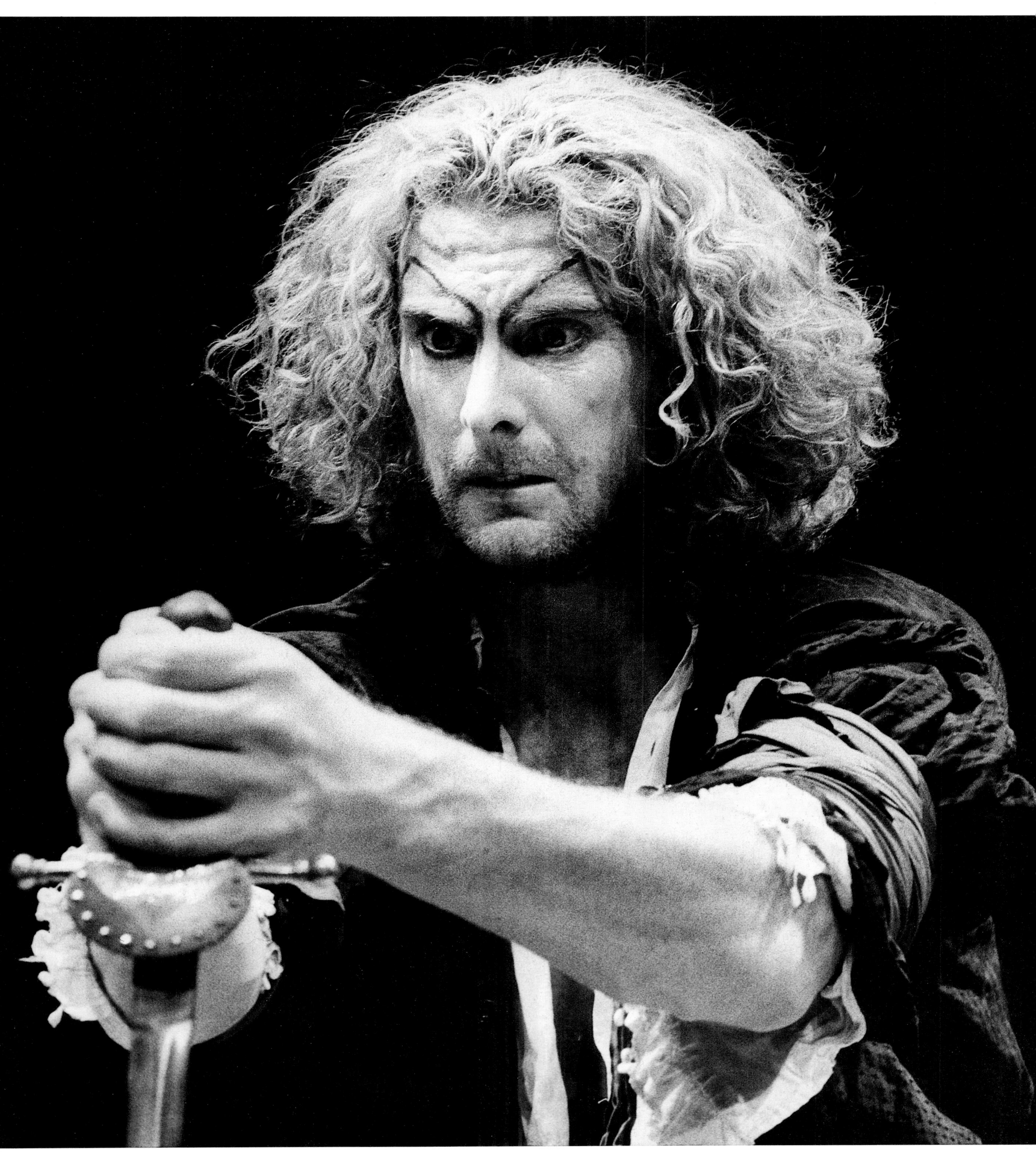

'HAMLET' | OXFORD PLAYERS | 1986

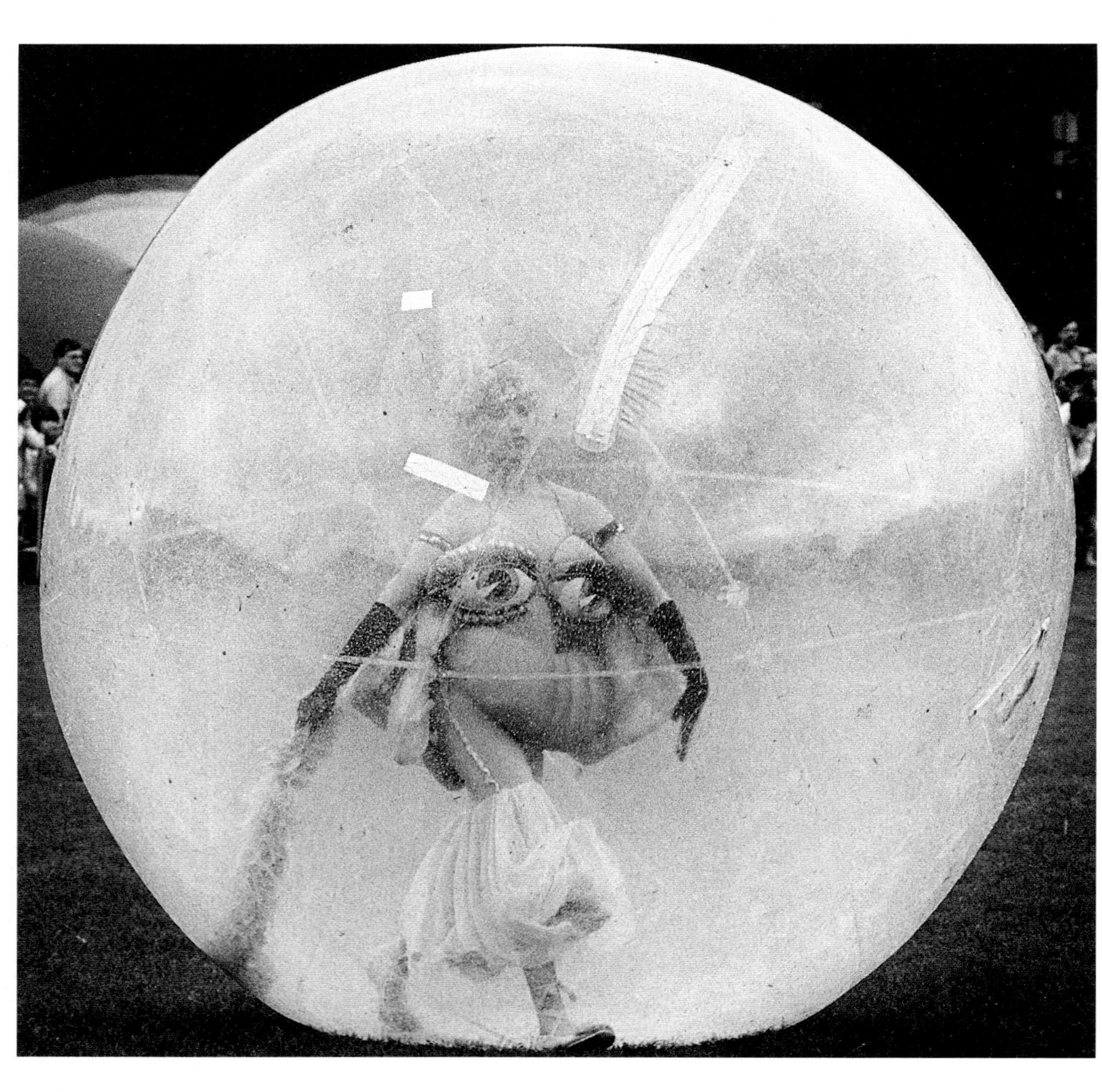

'SPHERES OF INFLUENCE' | MANCHESTER ARTS AND TECHNOLOGY WORKSHOP | FRINGE SUNDAY | 1985

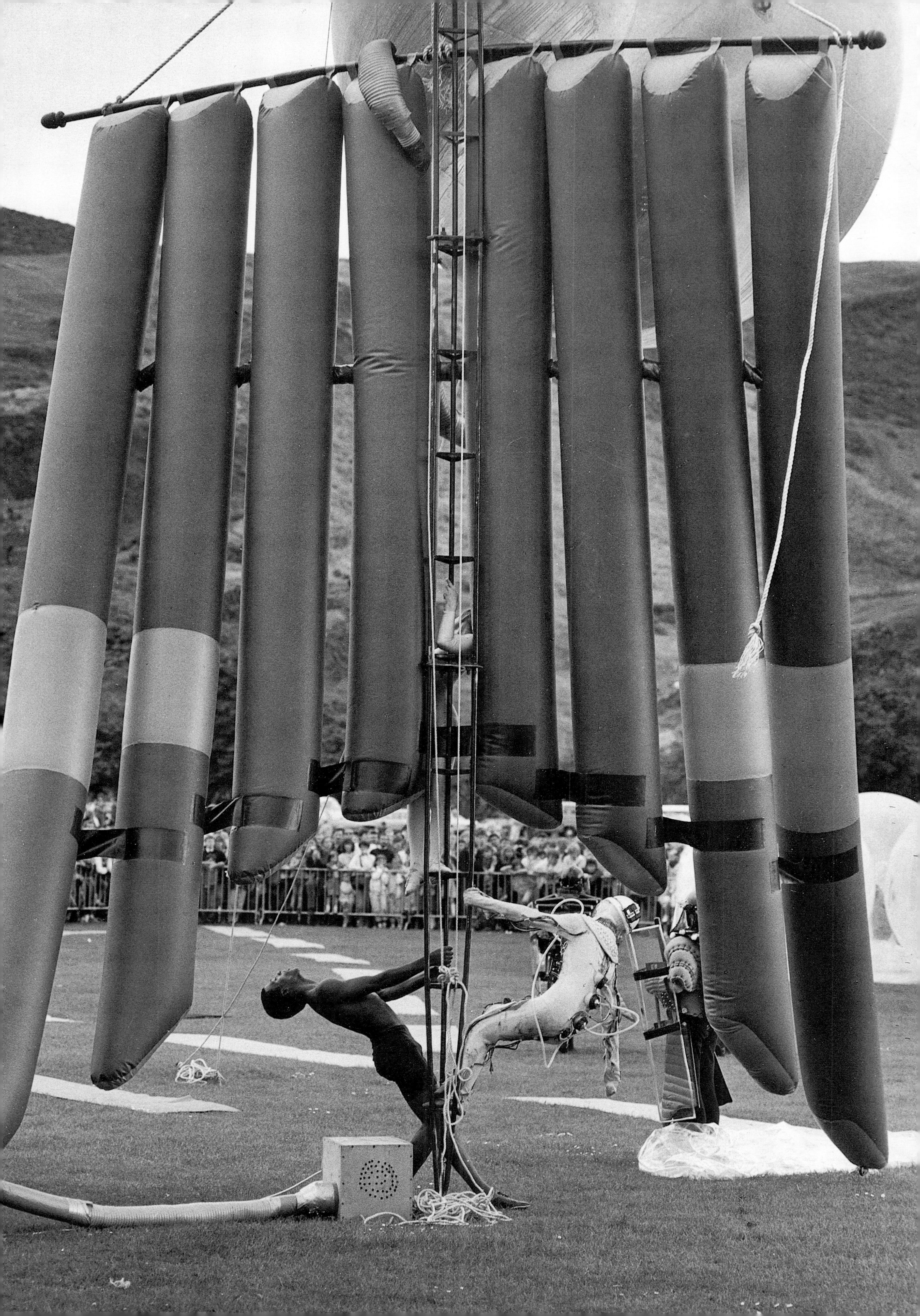

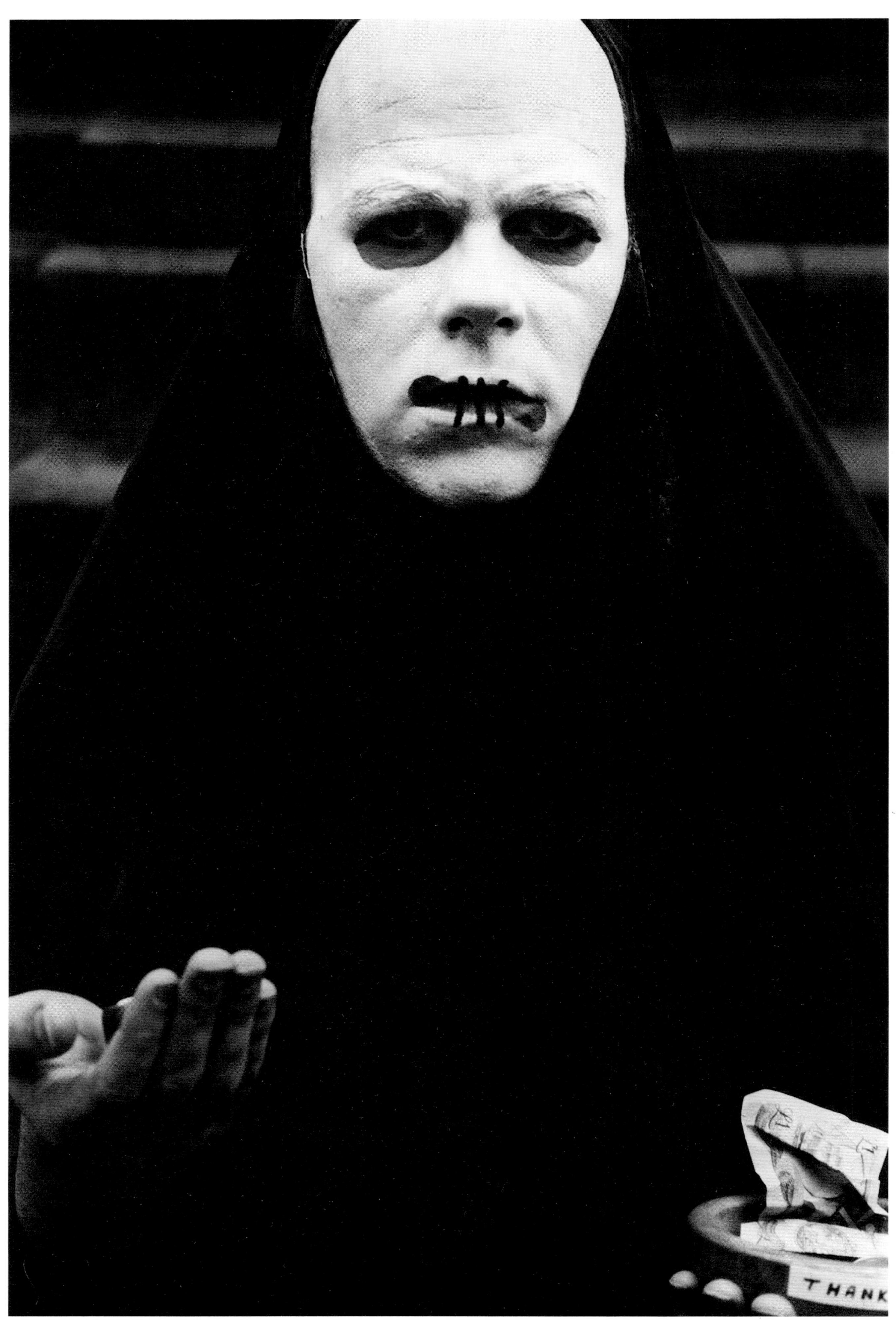

THE BEGGAR | 1984

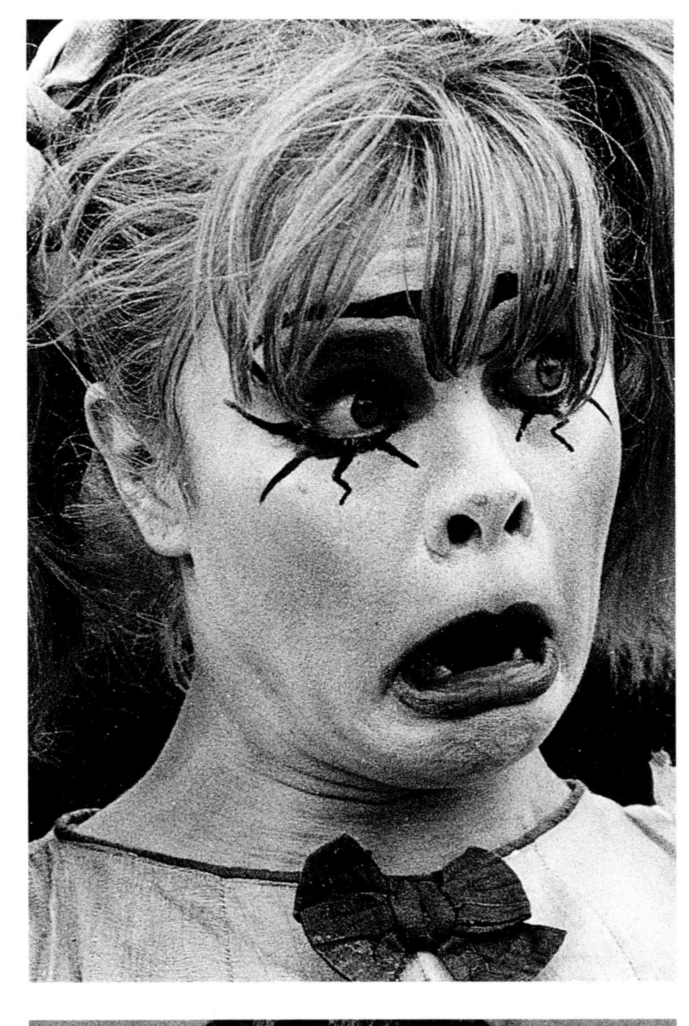

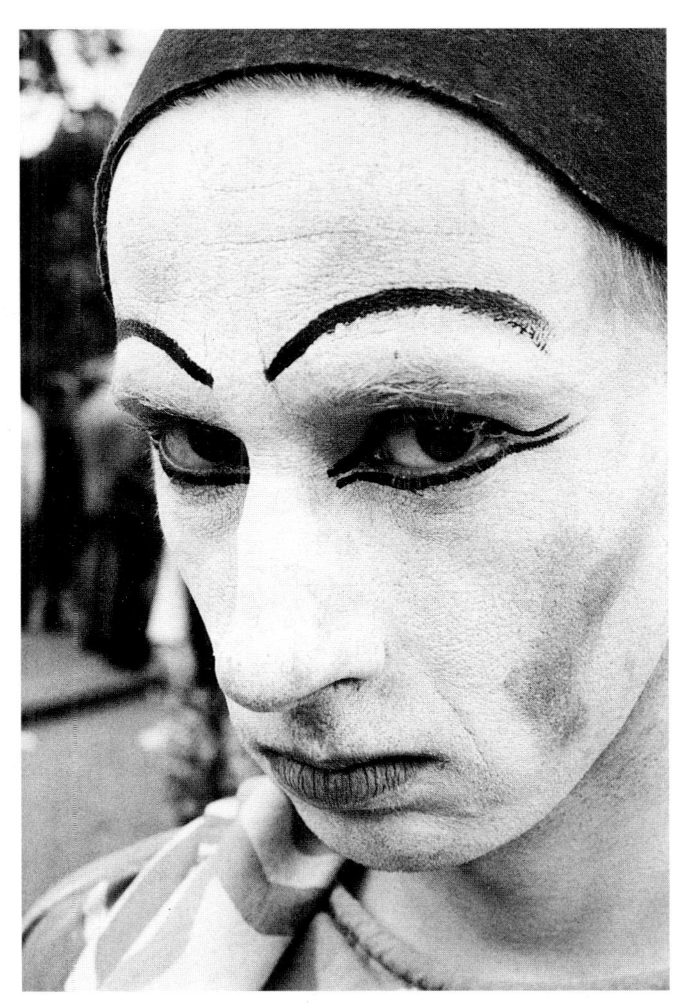

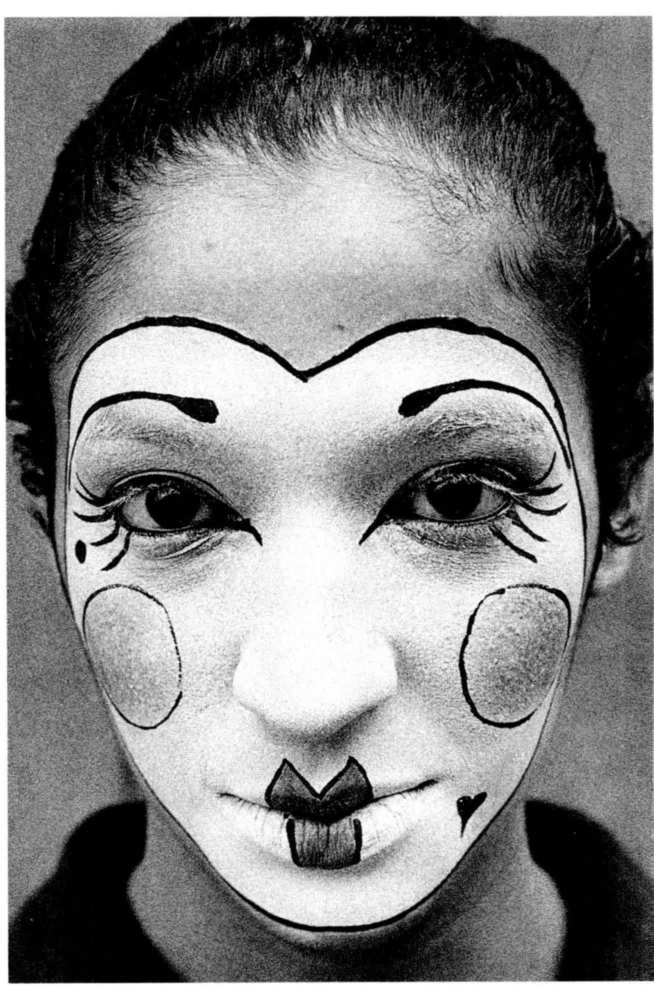

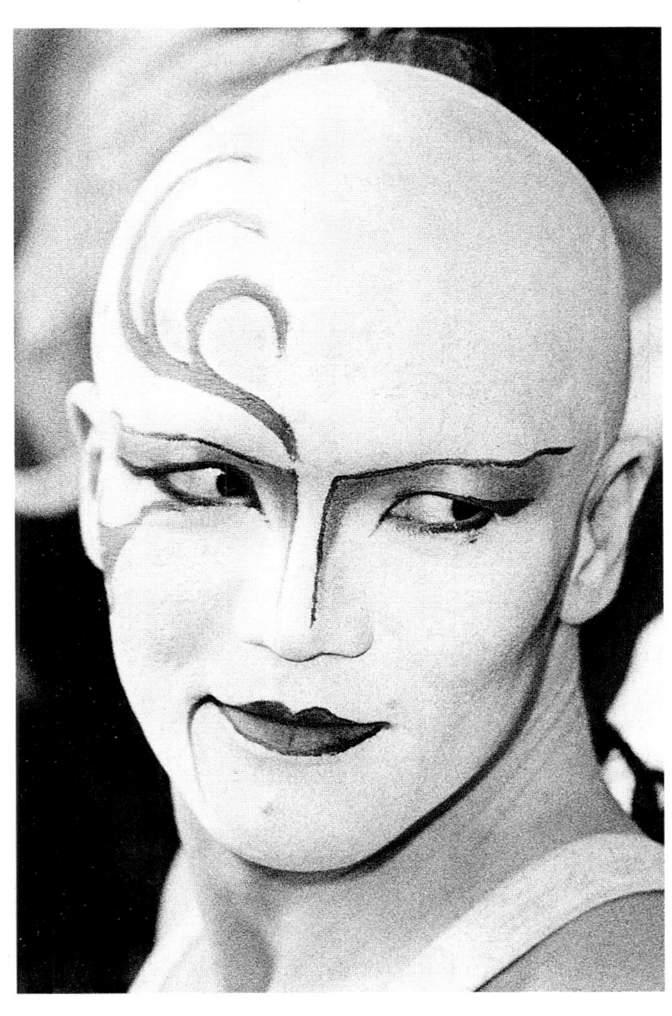

THE RAG DOLL | 1985

THE FOOL | 1985

THE CLOWN | 1986

THE SMILE | 1986

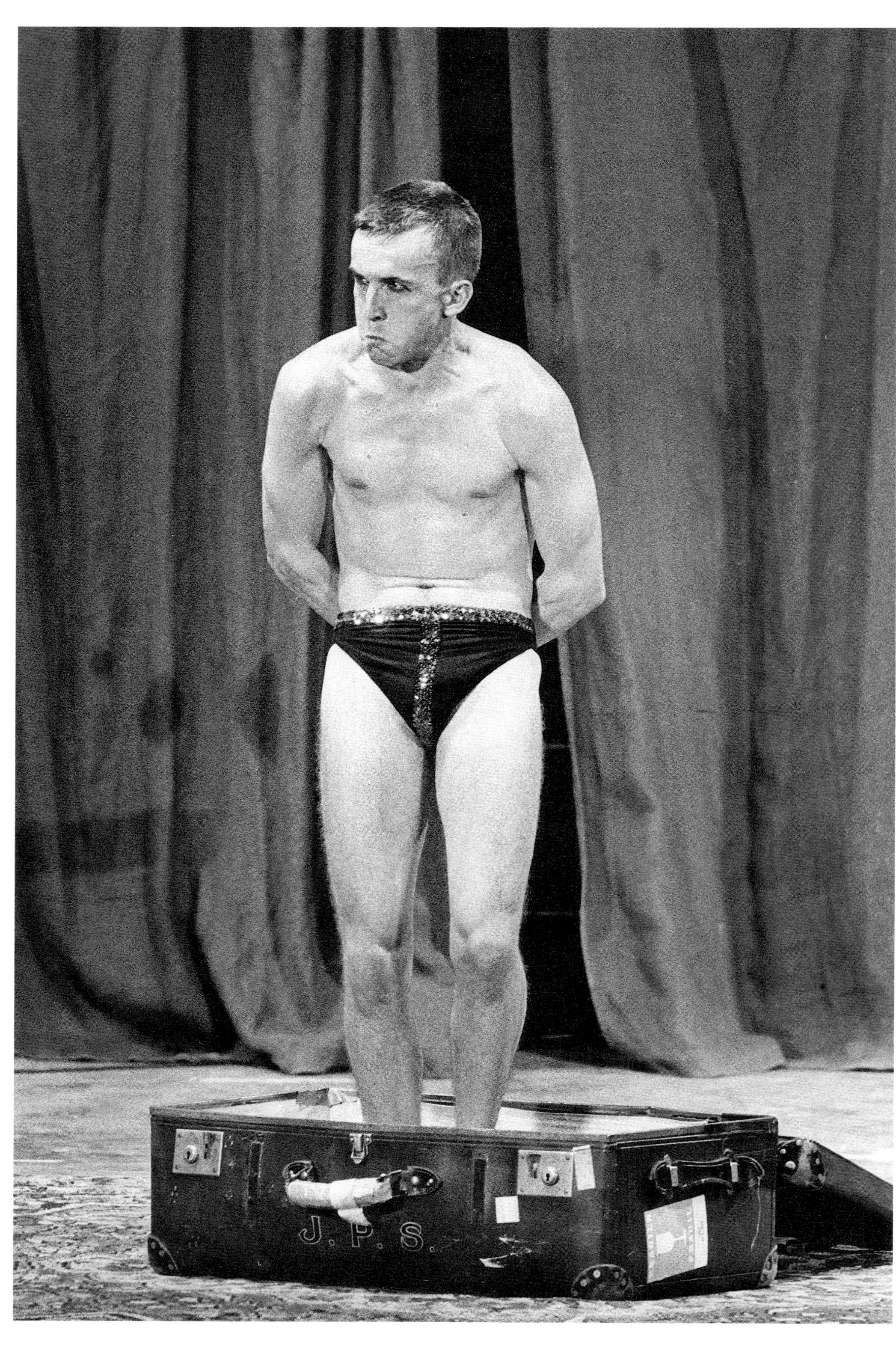

MAN IN A SUITCASE | RA RA ZOO | 1986

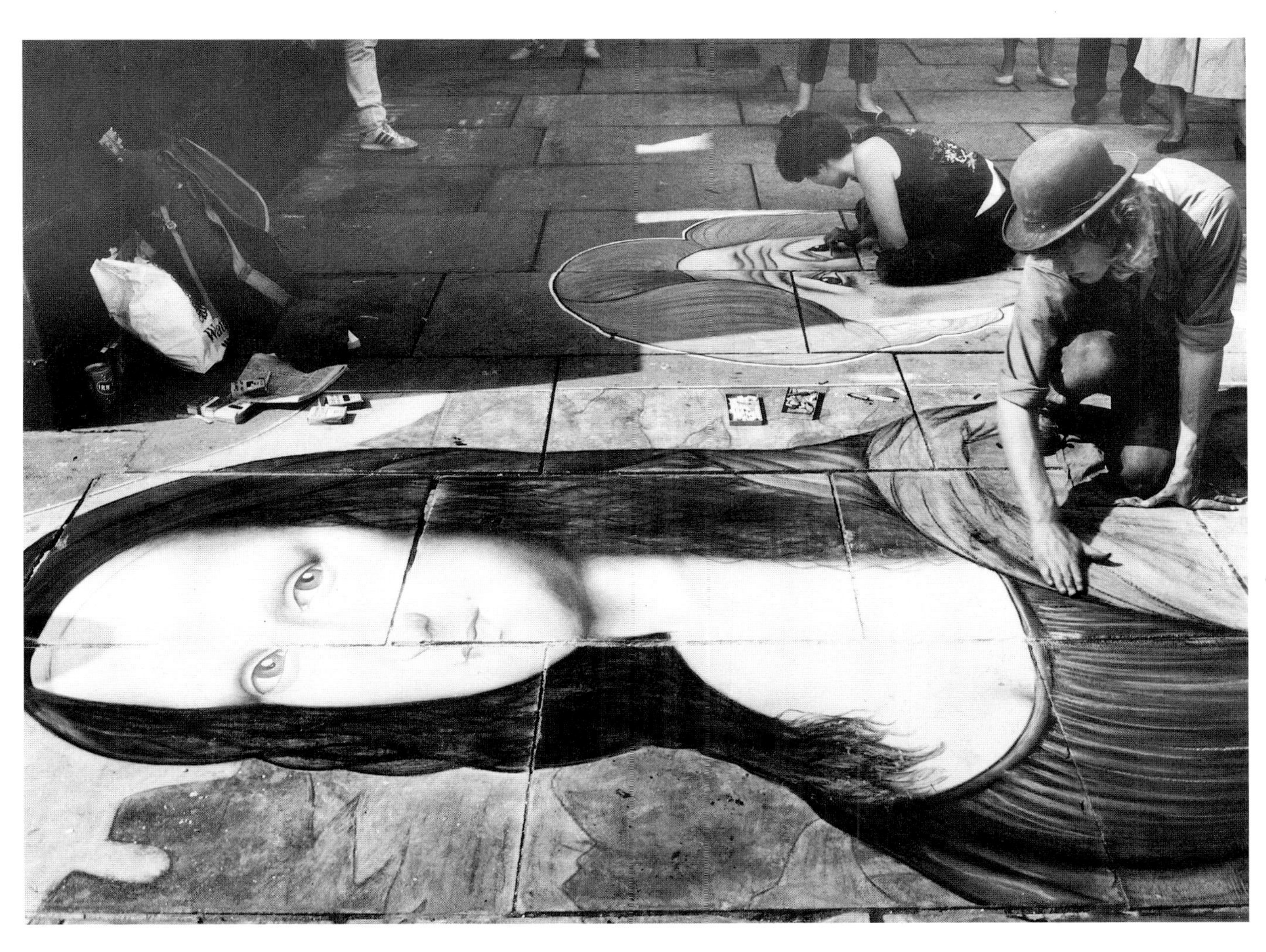

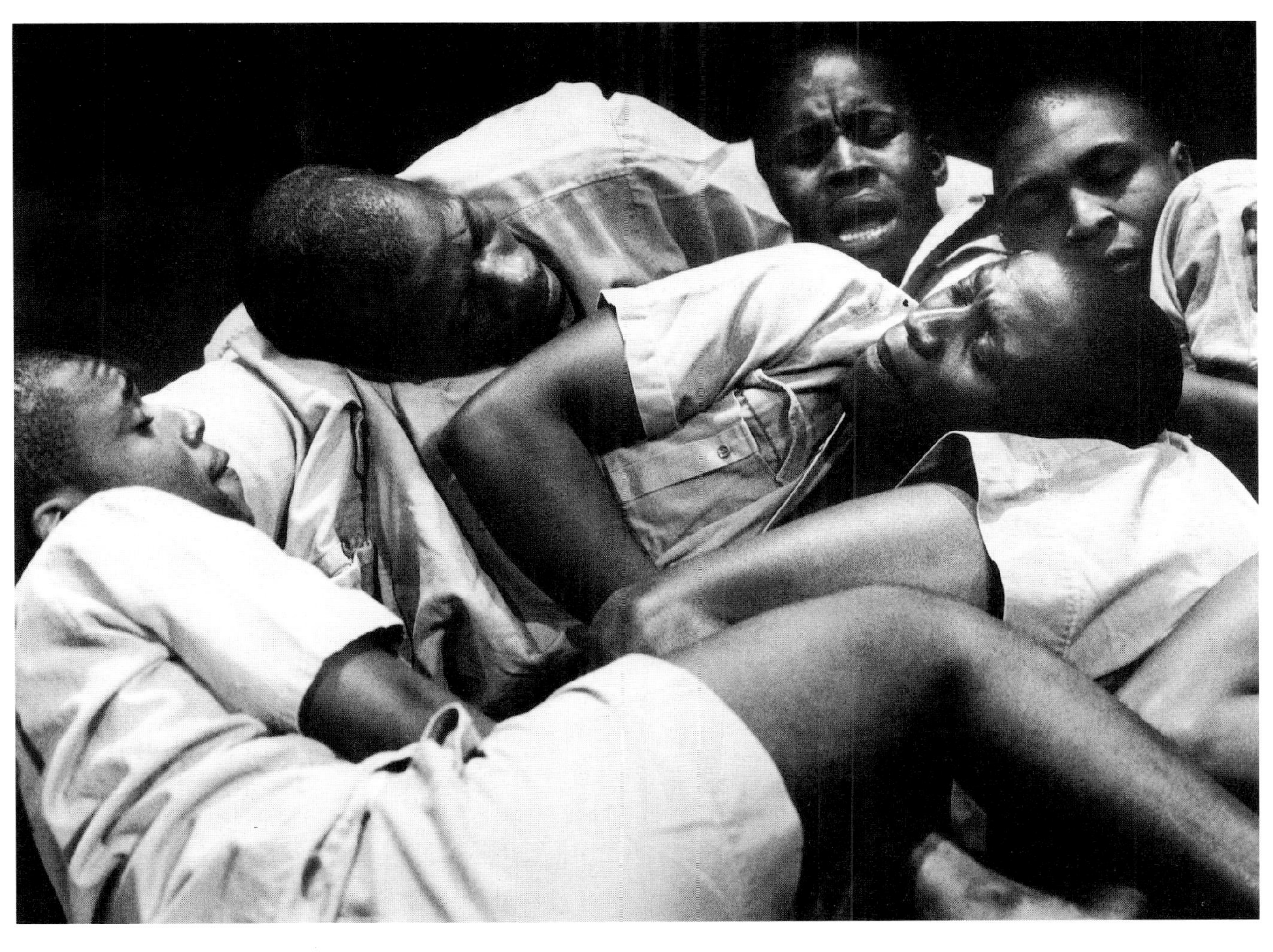

PAVEMENT ARTISTS | THE MOUND | 1984

MARKET THEATRE OF JOHANNESBURG | 1986

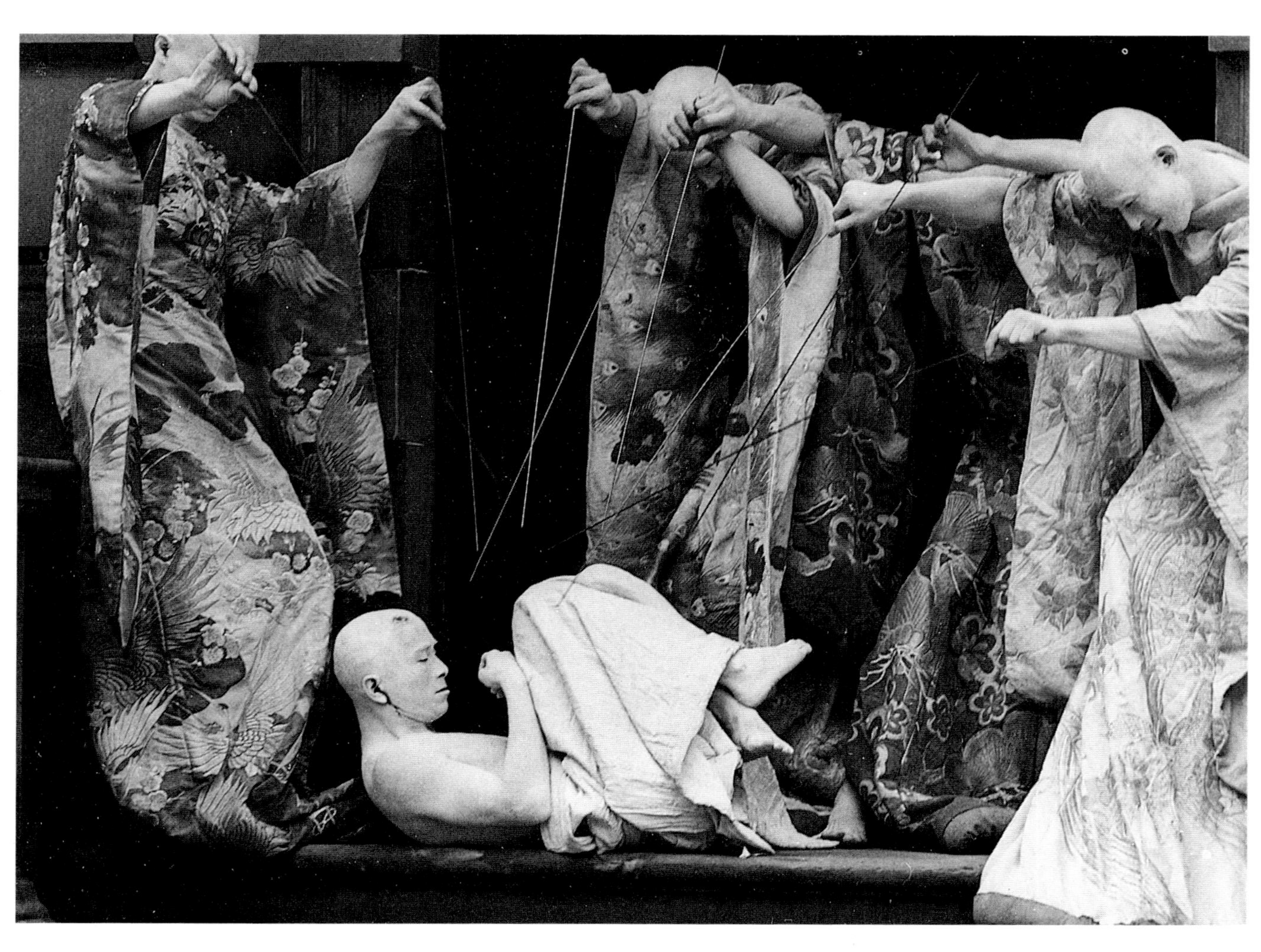

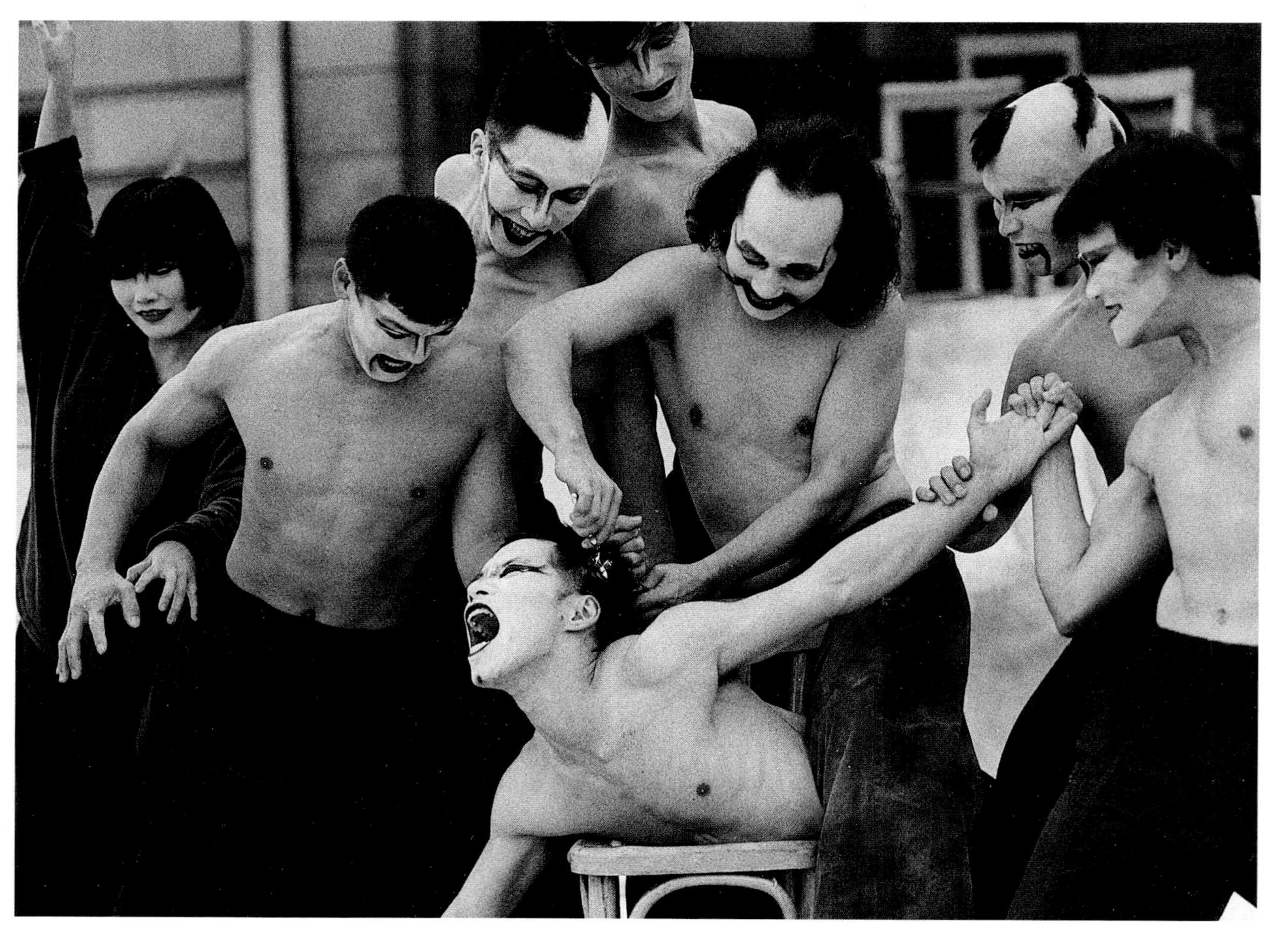

SANKAI JUKU | 1982 | TOP

'DESERT ZOO' | BAN'YU INRYOKU | 1986

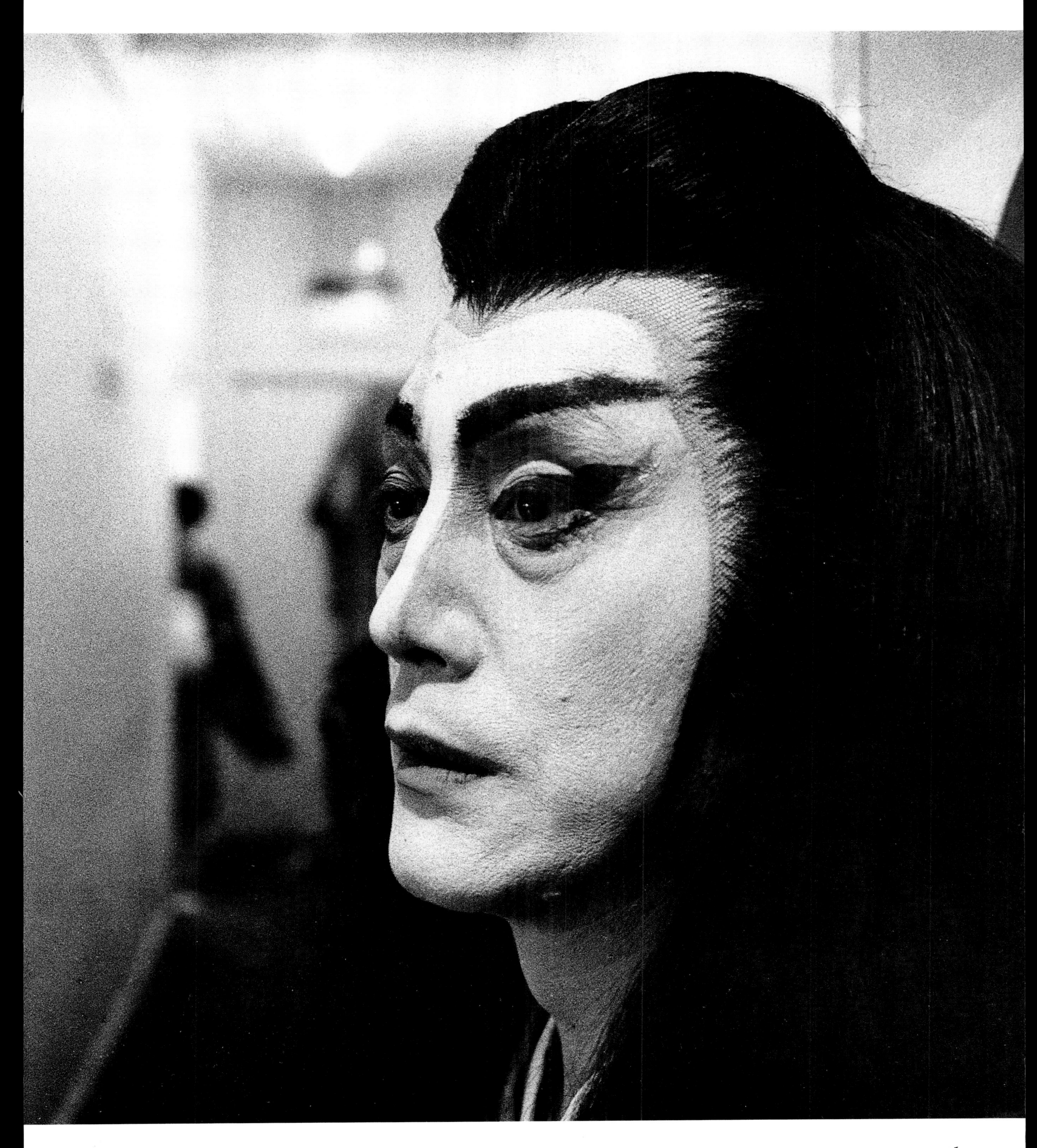

MIKIJIRO HIRA AS MACBETH | TOHO COMPANY | 1985

SANKAI JUKU | PARLIAMENT SQUARE | 1982 | NEXT PAGE

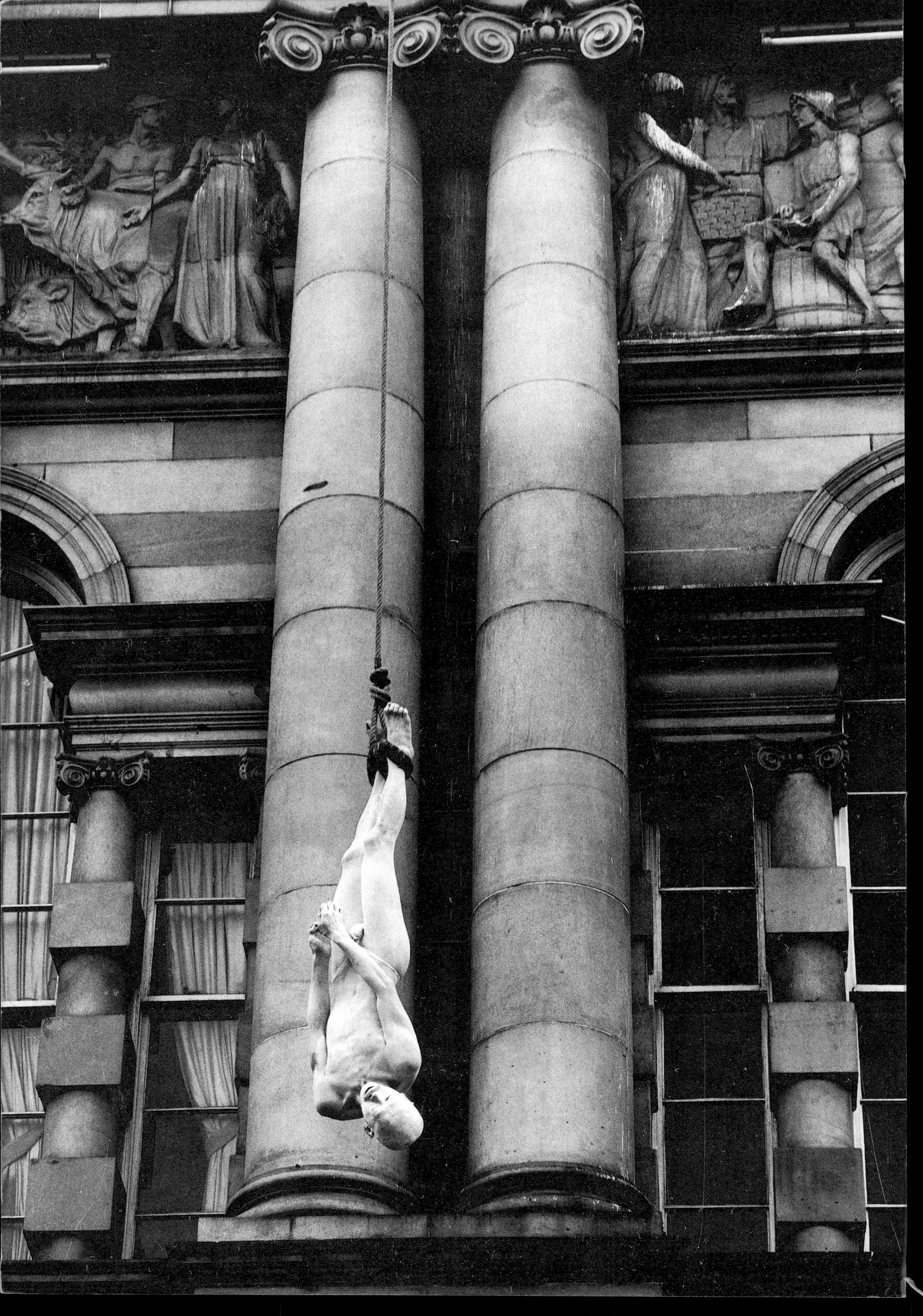